P9-BHR-685

At the Heart of the Whirlwind

John P. Adams

AT THE HEART OF THE WHIRLWIND

HARPER & ROW, PUBLISHERS

New York, Hagerstown, San Francisco, London

 For information address Harper & Row, Publishers, Inc., 10 East 53rd Street, New York, N.Y. 10022. Published simultaneously in Canada by Fitzhenry & Whiteside Limited, Toronto.

FIRST EDITION

Library of Congress Cataloging in Publication Data

Adams, John P 1923–
At the heart of the whirlwind.

1. Adams, John P., 1923– 2. Radicalism—United States. I. Title.
BX8495.A414A34 1976 287'.6'0924[B] 75-9343
ISBN 0-06-060080-2

---

76 77 78 79 10 9 8 7 6 5 4 3 2 1

For Rebecca and Martha . . .

and in memory of

Kenneth M. Adams, my nephew–

November 9, 1953–November 12, 1975

Contents

Preface

This book is about ministry in the midst of social conflict.

Immediately after World War II, Pastor Martin Niemöeller, a well-known German clergyman imprisoned for opposing policies of the Nazi government, described the role of the church in the age of nuclear warfare as "walking the last few steps with civilization." Perhaps, he suggested, all that was left for the church to do was to act as chaplain to a humanity shuffling toward execution.

In the 1950s we in the American church, for the most part, worked as chaplains to a society which seemed to be eating its last large meal before walking bravely toward a quick death in a nuclear holocaust.

But the bombs were not dropped. The ultimate weapons were not used, and civilization survived to face the 1960s and the 1970s. Instead of meeting death, the American people had to confront radical change. Rather than offering comfort to a society soon to die, the church was called upon to furnish courage to a society compelled to change.

Racial minorities called for long-delayed justice; idealistic youth opposed participation of the United States in a civil war in Southeast Asia. The church's ministry was strongly challenged to witness to the social implications of the gospel. Innumerable clergy and laity were literally called outside the church and into the world, beyond any previous concept of their ministries. Previously the parish had been their world. When the challenge came, the world became the parish.

St. Paul had once said that there was "a variety of ministries." In the social struggles and conflicts of the 1960s and the early 1970s, the total range of ministry was fully explored, often with great sacrifice and at high cost to many.

I had an opportunity to observe this "variety of ministry" as it was being performed in a time of rapid social change. For the past nine years I have worked as a liaison among social protest groups, church organizations, and agencies of the federal government. As a staff member of the national Board of Church and Society of the United Methodist Church, I have had continuing assignments which permitted me to be strongly identified with leaders of social protest organizations while simultaneously being closely related to government officials.

My primary assignment was conflict resolution and crisis intervention, and it required me to be present during a large number of confrontations. The essential task was to support nonviolent strategies of social protest by helping to identify specific grievances and offering options for action through opening lines of communication and response. After having pastored church congregations for more than fifteen years, I discovered that a pastoral role could be performed in the midst of social conflict. Just as in a local church congregation, this ministry called for interpreting the gospel, seeking the guidance of the Holy Spirit, developing trust, sharing moral insights, and retaining confidences. I observed many persons engaged in such a ministry in social conflict, and I began to participate in it.

Most frequently, the ministry involved social presence rather than social activism. The aggrieved speak for themselves when they have the opportunity. Those who need to hear the grievances are often more ready to listen in a forum supported by the church.

This book describes a number of events which have been significant in terms of effecting social justice in the United States. It tells of some ways in which Christian ministries were attempted in the midst of these events. Other events could easily have been included. It was impossible to recognize or even to name the many persons who were involved or who supported the ministries which I have attempted to describe. However, they sought no such recognition. They would agree with Robert Theobald: "You can have social change or you can get credit for social change, but you cannot have both."

1

Dramatic Performance or Urgent Message?

I had served Methodist congregations since 1948, and had assumed that my work as a pastor would continue—preaching sermons, visiting the sick, counseling those in trouble, being involved in the social issues of the local community, administering the program of a church. Then late in June, 1967, I was called to Washington, D.C. to become a staff member of the Board of Christian Social Concerns of the Methodist Church. (Now the Board of Church and Society of the United Methodist Church.) The change required a considerable shift in the concept of the ministry, but it was a ministry that was as fully centered in the gospel of Jesus Christ as the one which I endeavored to perform as a pastor. The implications of the gospel remain the same whether within the interactions of a local church or in the dynamics of the wider society. I was thrust into such a ministry without realizing what its hard requirements might be.

Leaving a pastorate in Hammond, Indiana, I arrived in time to participate in staff assignments throughout a summer filled with civil disorders, and began to see in Detroit, Newark and Milwaukee what I had only read about at the time of the Watts riot in 1965—broken windows, looted stores, and burned-out buildings. At night the sky was alight with flames, and smoke hung heavily over large sections of the cities. Police and National

Guard with military equipment dominated the streets. Helicopters chopped the air in tight surveillance as lights swept the streets and alleys during curfew hours. Gunfire was audible; tear gas smarted one's eyes.

Like most white Americans, I simply did not understand what was happening, but I tried to find out. Mrs. Rosa Parks talked to me in Detroit. Louis Lomax once said that the Negro revolt in America was born when Mrs. Rosa Parks refused to give up her seat to a white person on a bus in Montgomery, Alabama, on December 1, 1955. He called her the mother of the movement.

By the summer of 1967, Mrs. Parks had been a resident of Detroit for ten years. She lived where serious rioting took place and worked as a receptionist in the Detroit office of Congressman John Conyers. His office burned during the riot. He himself was shouted down from the top of an automobile when he attempted to address the restless people in the black community.

In an office which had been rapidly established in another building, I talked with Mrs. Parks about her feelings during the riot. She had watched with sadness the burning and the looting, for she knew that again it would be Negroes who would suffer as a result. She contrasted her reaction to the discrimination in Montgomery, Alabama, 1955, with the reaction of black citizens in Detroit, 1967. She had refused to give up her seat on the Montgomery bus because, "I was tired and I became angry." She worked long hours in her job as a seamstress and didn't see the sense in continuing to act out the ritual of discrimination. Comparing her anger in Montgomery to the anger in Detroit, she said, "Perhaps there is no difference. Maybe our anger is the same. In 1955, there were only a few of us. In those less-tense days, we were more patient. Now there are more who are angry, and they are not as patient. They are younger. They are willing to risk more."

I began to grasp the meaning of the events. Since we had failed to hear the anger of the patient, the hostility of the impatient roared around us. We did not understand this sufficiently in the white church. Some had started to stand up; most stood back. We began to take positions, but our commitment was tenuous. We had not kept pace with the nonviolent protests; consequently, we were completely out of step with what was taking place in black urban ghettos.

I thought of Søren Kierkegaard's parable about the actor who discovered the theater was on fire. He went on stage to warn people that they should leave as rapidly as possible. The audience, however, thought that what he was saying was merely part of his performance, and they applauded him. He warned them again and again, but each time they simply thought he was giving a better performance, and they applauded louder. As they cheered, the theater burned down, and they lost their lives.

We had marched on Washington in 1963. We had marched across the Edmund Pettis Bridge in Selma in 1965. We had supported nonviolent demonstrations of grievances, but in many ways it was as though we were applauding those on stage while the theater was on fire. We misinterpreted an urgent message as a dramatic performance, presented for the benefit of our democratic society.

Consequently, the summer of 1967 was aflame. During the month of July, more than one hundred disorders were reported in cities across the United States.

The board's headquarters in Washington was swamped with calls for assistance. Members of our staff, along with those of other denominations, fanned out to help. I was sent. At first there was little I could do but watch closely the work of clergy and laity in local communities responding to the riot crises. Under difficult and dangerous conditions, the church in action came through. In the pain and panic almost all institutions became paralyzed in some cities, but I saw the church continue to function and perform an essential role.

Back in Indiana, in the pastorate, I had watched churches respond to natural disasters. Congregations had collected money, food, and clothing, and volunteer work crews had assisted devastated areas. Church buildings had opened to house the stranded, and on short notice church kitchens were utilized to prepare meals in critical situations.

During the riots in 1967, I saw the church perform, not in a natural disaster, but in a social disaster. I was impressed with their courageous, immediate action. They not only met the human needs which surfaced during the riots, but they helped to identify the grievances which sparked the riots and caused them to proliferate. Through the churches, lines of communication were opened between disparate sections of metropolitan areas. Church members exerted influence upon public officials and supported community leaders.

There was a much needed blending of pastoral ministry and prophetic role as the church ministered during great danger and in the midst of vast destruction. The scene was changing rapidly for all parts of society, however, the church had a particular concern. Previously, congregations had debated extensively over the church's involvement in nonviolent protest and civil disobedience. Now the church was forced to confront violent actions, civil disorders, enormous human needs, and conflict. No one questioned whether the church should act, and I was able to observe the action.

When I returned to Washington, D.C., I attempted to describe the church in a crisis ministry in a booklet with the long descriptive title, "Guidelines for a Ministry of Compassion and Reconciliation by Laity and Clergy in the Riots in the Northern Urban Areas of the United States of America." It was distributed widely by the General Board of Christian Social Concerns of the Methodist Church.

In the introduction I wrote:

> There is a ministry to perform and there is a Christian witness to be made in this great crisis that is now facing our nation. The issues are firmly set upon the altar of the church. They cannot be avoided. We cannot shout down and we cannot shoot down those who are begnning to articulate the needs of the ghetto-ized communities. They have spoken with words and we did not listen. They are speaking now in ways that shock us, and the jolts have unstopped our ears. Let us be sure that we hear.
>
> This is a great tragedy for our nation, but just as the church in previous times of tragedy has found itself reshaped for service, so today,

we will discover that the church will be compelled to be the church and will be shaped to the task if it responds faithfully.

We were learning that violence can be a voice, a scream for help, and a hopeful, piercing cry ending with a deep sigh of despair. What was the church to be in a time of violence? The grand reconciler? At one time that might have been possible. Now the voice of violence was speaking as much to the church as to the rest of the society. It became apparent that one of the church's major efforts would be to make certain it did not sanction the forces of repression. Some never want to hear what the voices of protest are saying and are capable of unleashing a heavy force of retaliation when those who dissent become so desperate that they turn to even minor forms of violence. The lid is clamped on quickly. Voices are muffled and then silenced. When quiet is restored, presumably the problem is solved. But the church must not bless the violence of repression because of the dilemma presented by the violence of protest. Rather it must act as a sensitive listening device—catching the signals ahead of the violence whenever possible and translating them into messages which will be heard in the privileged and protected places of society. If violence comes, listening must be more intense, and deciphering, even more conscientious and persuasive.

I became convinced that in our society the church does not need to be a protest movement in and of itself. Those who suffer, who are neglected, those against whom there is discrimination, can and will speak for themselves. We must not take away their initiative but, in acceptable forums, support those who present their grievances to a society which can so easily ignore them. The church has a responsibility to use its resources in making available options for communicating those grievances. These platforms or channels may or may not be utilized by the groups seeking redress, but they ought to be offered, and, when accepted, they should be provided.

Nearly as important as identifying with those against whom society discriminates, I learned, is establishing and maintaining contact with those in official positions in governmental agencies which have the responsibility for relating to protest groups.

They can be receptive to the protest. They are also the persons who most directly feel political pressures from those parts of society which want protests silenced and who demand that governmental officials ignore voices of dissent.

Remember, those who are privileged and powerful do not have to engage in public protest. They can make phone calls to friends in high places, or they can write letters which will be given serious attention in influential offices. They can even engage in violence, but it will be so subtle and discreet that it will hardly be noticed. In contrast, the violence of the desperate is exposed and conspicuous, and it is, therefore, more vulnerable to disapproval and reaction.

We can be grateful for the number of public officials and law enforcement personnel who, within the last few years, have begun to take seriously their responsibility to protect the rights of all citizens to assemble and seek redress for their grievances. They have seen the protection of these rights as important as the protection of life and property. They have to maintain a delicate balance in the midst of social change, but many police administrators and public officials have clearly demonstrated that it can be done.

The church needs to support those officials and administrators who strive to respect the rights of those who protest and who are willing themselves to hear the voices of dissent. Our society depends upon the full functioning of the First Amendment—the right to assemble freely and speak. There are times when this is inconvenient, disturbing, and even expensive, but it is essential to a society which seeks justice for all citizens and attempts to secure their individual rights.

In the following pages I recount a ministry which sought to assist groups exercising their First Amendment rights and to support government officials and others who labored to respect those rights and respond to the grievances. It involved both pastoral and prophetic responsibilities.

2

Marches in Milwaukee

"That priest is violent and irrational!" spluttered the Milwaukee mayor, Henry W. Maier, in September, 1967. Father James E. Groppi, a white priest, served in a black section of the city as assistant pastor of St. Boniface Catholic Church. The community was cut up by urban renewal (termed urban "removal" by the blacks) and scarred by the riots. The priest's "irrationality" consisted of growing up in an ethnic neighborhood on the south side of Milwaukee and now identifying with the grievances of the city's black core. Some saw his close relationship to the Milwaukee NAACP Youth Council, of which he was an adviser, as equaling violence.

The battle between the Milwaukee municipal government and the NAACP Youth Council began when the youth council supported a proposed fair-housing ordinance introduced in the Milwaukee Common council by Mrs. Vel Phillips, the only black member of the city's legislative body. The measure was repeatedly defeated but, to the city's embarrassment, regularly reintroduced by Mrs. Phillips.

A riot broke out in Milwaukee on July 30–31. One of the many disturbances of the summer of 1967, it seemed to be a fall-out from the Detroit civil disorder. Milwaukee police were tense, and the NAACP Youth Council hoped to channel community anger into a constructive project by massing black support for the fair-housing ordinance. This would dramatize the grievances of citizens dislocated by urban renewal projects and who, because of unwritten restrictions, were shut out of other housing except in neighborhoods being "tipped" from white to black through exploitation by certain real estate agents.

The NAACP Youth Council initiated nightly fair-housing marches on August 28, 1967. Long columns of blacks, predominantly young, moved out of their communities into other sections of the city. They marched peacefully but repeatedly chanted demands for the fair-housing ordinance. The city administration used diverse tactics to restrict the demonstrations, discredit the movement, and smother any support that it received. Nevertheless, the youth council kept marching.

White resistance mounted; marchers were attacked when they moved out of the black section. Police often times intimidated the marchers rather than protected them. Bloody confrontations took place.

The NAACP Youth Council formed a highly disciplined paramilitary corps called the Commandoes. They were trained and assigned to protect marchers from any assaults by white citizenry or police. Whites marched on the chancery of the Most Reverend William E. Cousins, archbishop of Milwaukee, and demanded Father Groppi's removal. Politicians pressured the archbishop. Letters poured into the chancery denouncing him as "cowardly," "stupid," "blind and weak," for refusing to transfer the priest out of St. Boniface.

Archbishop Cousins answered those who demanded that Father Groppi be "defrocked," "have his collar torn off," "be suspended," "sent to Africa," in the archdiocesan paper, the *Catholic Herald Citizen.* In an editorial, he asked, "Do you honestly believe that Father Groppi's absence from the scene would somehow miraculously heal all wounds, and cure all social ills? The underlying cases of unrest, pointed up by the Youth Council, would go on plaguing us. They existed long before Father Groppi's advent."

A city newspaper warned that Milwaukee teetered "on the

edge of madness." The latent resistance exploded after only two weeks of marches. Other churches began to be involved. The Inner Core Cadre of Clergy, composed of urban and metropolitan ministers of all the major denominations, joined with the NAACP Youth Council to ask for support from the religious community outside Milwaukee. They invited clergy and laity from across the nation to take part in the marches, beginning September 16. The Greater Milwaukee Council of Churches Executive Committee endorsed the invitation, and the General Board of the National Council of Churches, meeting at the time in Atlanta, passed a resolution supporting it.

Hundreds of clergy and laity came for the weekend. Church executives from eight denominations and from the National Council of Churches marched in lines led by Father Groppi, Mrs. Vel Phillips, and the top-ranking officers of the NAACP Youth Council Commandoes.

I marched with the Commandoes for the first time on that weekend. When the national staff returned to their offices because of other responsibilities, my assignment was to stay and continue to relate to the Milwaukee movement. I attended every rally, marched night after night, and then in the daytime kept in telephone contact with the National Council of Churches staff both in New York and in the central states field office in Chicago. Each day I interpreted the turn of events to staff persons of our own and other denominations.

I marched in the back of the lines, had no contact with the Commando officers, and had never met Father Groppi personally. From my position, this seemed to be a different kind of movement. Signs proclaimed "Black and White Together." "Black Power, Black Power, Black Power!" was chanted. Stokley Carmichael's words shouted on the James Meredith March against Fear in Mississippi in 1966 were full-throatedly asserted.

In press conferences the Commandoes qualifyingly stated that they were tactically nonviolent. Nonviolence was not to be exploited, they made clear. Although unarmed, they were physically prepared to defend the marches from any attempts to break the lines or to injure the marchers. Wearing military insignia on their sweatshirts, they led us through hostile crowds, shielded us from rocks and bottles, and outmaneuvered the aggressive actions of police. Everyone who marched was expected to follow directions and be nonviolent. There was no question about who was in charge.

One night one of my shoelaces became untied. I stepped out of line to tie it. No sooner had I stooped down than a Commando was at my side, ordering me back in the line—very firmly. Thereafter, whenever I had an emergency, I signaled to one of the Commandoes who patroled the lines, and asked permission.

As I marched each night, I came to know the Commandoes individually. After some time, I met Father Groppi. Some trust seemed to develop. One morning I was asked to come to the rectory of St. Boniface church where some of the Commando officers reported new and increased pressure placed upon Archbishop Cousins to remove Father Groppi. They suggested that I go to the archbishop and intepret the movement as I had seen it. The dismissal of Father Groppi would mean trouble, they warned. Dr. Harold Weaver, pastor of Wauwatosa Methodist Church, who had worked with the archbishop in ecumenical projects, arranged the appointment, and we went together to the chancery.

The leader of the seven hundred thousand Catholics in the ten-county Milwaukee archdiocese listened attentively at length and responded with real kindness. Two Protestant clergymen talking with a Catholic archbishop about transferring one of his priests could surely seem impertinent. Nevertheless, I spoke earnestly about the importance of Father Groppi's remaining at St. Boniface. The archbishop said he knew that, but he also had to consider the loss of tens of thousands of dollars of income which had been incurred in the archdiocese as a result of Father Groppi's close relationship to the NAACP Youth Council. He spoke of his responsibility to the church institutions in the area—hospitals, schools, welfare agencies. But he said that he would make every effort to keep Father Groppi at St. Boniface. I must have spoken rather passionately, for as I left, the archbishop, after thanking us for coming, said, "You're a kind of Methodist Father Groppi, I believe."

After that meeting Dr. Weaver and I discussed ways in which we could relieve the political pressure on the archbishop even if the financial problems were beyond our reach. I suggested that we ask Ralph Taylor Alton, the Methodist bishop of Wisconsin, to come to St. Boniface and march with Father Groppi and the Commandoes. Bishop Alton was also the president of the Wisconsin Council of Churches; this would symbolize influential local concern in addition to national religious support. Bishop Alton had previously expressed strong backing for the fair-housing proposals and had written a letter to all Methodist churches in Wisconsin to this effect. He agreed to march that next Saturday at 3:00 P.M. Telephone calls bombarded Bishop Alton's home, and critical letters poured into his office. He and his wife decided to leave their house until time for him to be at St. Boniface. He marched, and some of the fire was drawn from the archbishop. Father Groppi remained.

It became apparent that participating in a protest, supporting it, passing resolutions, and so on was important, but the church had to play another role—a brokering, facilitating one. This could not be imposed on a movement, but I was convinced that it ought to be tactfully offered, and if accepted, no matter how reluctantly, it should be vigorously but discreetly worked. For a grievance to be surfaced, and be identified, dramatized and channeled, many behind-the-scenes efforts were needed. They were ones with which several national denominational offices could assist. We did not have to wait for riots to communicate to us and our churches.

Still I kept marching every night and felt more physically fit than at any time since I had been in the military service. During the day, with local religious leadership, I contacted the municipal government, addressed organizations and raised funds. On one occasion, Mrs. Phillips and I called on a newspaper editor whose paper had consistently editorialized against the housing marches. We must have given him a new perspective, for within days, the paper had this to say: "Milwaukee is experiencing an arousal of its citizenry toward a political goal, a mobilization of community forces, in demand for open housing legislation. Such a movement is without precedent in our times. Our timid or reluctant public officials have never seen anything like it—and it is still growing in both scope and the intensity of its expression . . . Milwaukee must put itself in a right posture now, with municipal law, whatever may follow in other jurisdictions."

The Common Council continued to vote against Mrs. Phillips' proposed ordinance. Fair housing in the North was as delicate an issue as black voter registration and nondiscriminatory public accommodations in the South.

Milwaukee was at a political stalemate. I made several contacts back in Washington through the assistance of the Community Relations Service of the United States Department of Justice. I met one of its field representatives on the street in Milwaukee. This unique agency of the federal government, created by the Civil Rights Act of 1964, was designed to help communities cope effectively with "disputes, disagreements, or difficulties relating to discriminatory practices based on race, color, or national origin . . ." (42 USC 2000 g–1).

At first, I could not grasp the significance of the work of this agency. As part of the Department of Justice, it did not investigate crimes or enforce laws. It could not receive funding proposals or make grants of money for community programs. Its work focused completely on opening lines of communication between dissenting groups and various government agencies. Its mandate was conciliation.

CRS field personnel worked with a responsible flexibility, and, I noticed, they seemed to have sufficient trust both among movement leaders and governmental officials to be able to suggest alternatives in tight and potentially violent situations. Here was a vitally needed service. CRS field representatives were not government infiltrators. They were clearly identified by the Commandoes. Neither did CRS personnel sabotage local government which, similarly, knew of their functioning. It was a working link, and there were few that did work in the circumstances.

The Milwaukee fair-housing movement could effect federal open-housing legislation which had been filibustered to death in the United States Senate in 1966. It occurred to me that a well-planned trip to Washington, D.C., by a group of Commandoes and Father Groppi might mobilize support back in Milwaukee as well. I asked CRS whether it would help to set up strategic appointments if the NAACP Youth Council requested them, and they responded positively.

I called the youth council, saying there was a possible national strategy for them to consider. They told me to come to St. Boniface Church and wait outside a phone booth. A few minutes after I arrived, a young man in a Commando sweatshirt accompanied me into a downstairs back room of the church. When I entered, Father Groppi and ten Commandoes, only two of whom I had seen before, were present. Not only were their faces new to me, their military insignia were of higher rank than those I had seen on the street. They told me to state my case. I reported on my contacts and the possibilities of appointments in Washington. Several denominational agencies could probably raise funds to pay for the travel expenses of a small group. The Commandoes discussed the prospect among themselves; Father Groppi was not asked for nor did he give his opinion. Finally, it was agreed that five Commandoes and three other persons, one of whom would be Father Groppi, would go if I could complete the arrangements. I was dismissed from the meeting.

Within ten days, two different groups of Commandoes went to Washington along with Mrs. Phillips, the black member of the Milwaukee Common Council; Father Groppi; Father Patrick Flood, executive director of the Council on Urban Affairs of the Archdiocese of Milwaukee; and Rev. David Owen, chairman of the Inner Core Cadre of Ministers.

Appointments and conferences with a number of senators and congressmen and federal department officials, all of whom had been suggested by the NAACP Youth Council as persons they wanted to see, were arranged by George Culberson of the Community Relations Service and Monsignor Geno Baroni of the archdiocese of Washington. The appointments were so closely scheduled that the group kept running behind, arriving late for meetings with some very important people. Yet, members of Congress and federal officials were always waiting when they arrived. At last, someone was listening.

One afternoon, long after most offices were closed, the Commandoes arrived very late for an appointment with Senator Walter Mondale, sponsor of the federal fair-housing bill. In the midst of a long discussion, I heard Senator Mondale tell the Commandoes that the country owed them a debt of gratitude for helping to keep the open-housing matter before the nation. "Except for you," he said, "the issue would be absolutely dead. Yet it is one which the country has to face, for it lies at the base of so many other problems of closed opportunity and deep discrimination, especially in the North. If the bill ever passes, it will be because of you." No one before had ever expressed appreciation to the Commandoes for their terribly demanding and dangerous work.

While we were in Washington, black nationalists contacted the Commandoes. The Milwaukee NAACP Youth Council was criticized for allowing a white priest to advise them. For nearly twenty-four hours, real conflict raged behind the scenes. One of the Commandoes said that he wanted to see Stokley Carmichael personally to go over the situation. I called Mr. Carmichael, and he told me to come with the Commando to a shoeshine parlor off 14th Street early the next morning. After introducing them, I started to leave, but Stokley signaled me to stay. I heard an interesting exchange about the real meaning of Black Power which supported what was happening in Milwaukee.

The next day, the Commandoes held a press conference in the chapel of the Methodist Building on Captiol Hill. The top-ranking officer said, "Father Groppi and ourselves are together. We would die together, even if it meant going to hell. This movement is black and white. It contains people of all colors. We do not turn anyone away who is seeking justice for blacks and who is willing to work and sacrifice to bring it into existence."

Dick Gregory put it another way at a rally back in St. Boniface Church: "What you're doing here in Milwaukee is convincing a lot of cats that Black Power is dependent, not upon color, but on attitude."

The Milwaukee fair-housing marches seemed anachronistic to those blacks who after the riots believed that violence had communicated far more effectively with the white power structure than any demonstrations and marches. Actually, the Milwaukee marches helped many white persons come to a real understanding of the necessity of exerting Black Power. It was a conclusion that could not have been reached in a fully violent setting. The very words, *Black Power* were so threatening in the summer and fall of 1967 that some mechanism was needed for translating them into a white awareness. Thc Milwaukee marches were one means by which that translation was made to some.

Appeals for integration were largely ignored. Eruptions of violence led to repressive resistance. Black Power was the necessary alternative, and in Milwaukee it was expressed in a form which was provocative without being destructive. It was educational.

Politically, the fair-housing marches probably influenced the federal fair-housing legislation to the point that it was ready and available for consideration and passage when Dr. King was slain. The congressional climate was suddenly receptive, and a vote was taken on the legislation.

Milwaukee Commandoes marched nearly three hundred nights and days before passage of the federal legislation. One of the last marches was held on the day of Dr. King's funeral, April 9, 1968. The 1968 Civil Rights Act was finally approved on April 10.

A few months later, the staff report of the Task Force on Law Enforcement of the National Advisory Commission on the Causes and Prevention of Violence described Father James E. Groppi as a "bridge-builder." It drew a parallel between the role which the church effectively performed in helping European immigrants to adjust in a new land, and the role which the church needs to play in supporting Black, Puerto Rican, and Mexican people as they seek a sense of community, social solidarity, and personal worth in the United States. Father Groppi was doing for blacks what the church had done for former residents of the inner cities.

3

Elections in Gary

Less than five months after I had left Hammond, Indiana, I was back in Lake County assigned to relate to the mayoral election in Gary. I was not there to campaign for a particular person, although the activity in which I and others engaged could have been interpreted as support for Richard Gordon Hatcher, Jr., the Democratic candidate.

Mr. Hatcher, an honors graduate of Valparaiso University School of Law and a member of the Gary City Council for four years, was not only campaigning against his Republican opponent, Joseph Radigan, but also against the Lake County Democratic organization. The organization had refused to support Mr. Hatcher. Mr. Hatcher is black.

Saying that "Gary is not ready for a Negro mayor," John C. Krupa, county Democratic chairman, would not furnish the customary party financial support for Hatcher's campaign. Krupa actually campaigned openly for Mr. Radigan, claiming that Hatcher would not publicly denounce certain black extremists, including Stokley Carmichael and H. Rap Brown. Hatcher replied, "I'm opposed to anyone who advocates violence. Krupa has a long list of people—including Marlon Brando—he wants me to denounce. And if I denounce them today, he'd have a whole new list tomorrow. He wouldn't support me if I stood on my head."

The Democratic county chairman continued to fire charges at the Democratic candidate: Hatcher's whole organization was subversive; if Hatcher were elected, there was the danger of a leftist takeover. One Democratic party worker in Gary disassociated himself from the smear tactics and expressed his enlightened disgust with the comment, "For Krupa, to be black is to be red."

The theme of black extremism and radicalism was played heavily among ethnic populations, concentrations of Polish, Slavic, and Czech particularly strong on Gary's south side. Widely distributed campaign literature contained inflammatory comments about the black candidate.

The Lake County Democratic machine had for years automatically produced victories for its mayoral candidates. Its mechanism was adjusted so that it could elect a Republican mayor while producing Democratic winners for all other offices, a peculiarly bipartisan and racist victory.

The Hatcher for Mayor organization purchased full-page advertisements in the New York *Times* and the Gary *Post Tribune*, appealing for contributions. More than forty thousand dollars came in.

The Lake County Election Board, which Mr. Krupa as county clerk chaired, purged voter registration rolls in black precincts. At the same time, thousands of false names were added to registration rolls in white precincts.

Hatcher's committee sent a telegram to the attorney general of the United States, Ramsey Clark, claiming that Hatcher would be cheated out of an election: "We have absolute and undeniable proof that certain prominent election officials are engaged in massive fraudulent registrations in white areas in order to steal the election. At the same time, they are wantonly and illegally disenfranchising thousands of Negroes who are qualified and registered to vote. We charge that no protection is given our candidate by the members of both political parties who comprise the registration and election boards."

The city was on the edge of violence as frustration grew in the black community. Efforts of black citizens to use the electoral process were being illegally thwarted. Thousands of National

Guard troops assembled in areas within fifteen minutes of the city. Police activated contingency plans. Clergymen within Gary also took initiatives to reduce the potential for violent confrontation. At this point I was asked to come to the city.

We set up a center in the basement of City Methodist Church, enlisted volunteers, formulated strategy, and carefully laid plans.

Working closely with ministers, priests, and rabbis, most of whom I knew well, I recommended that we check voter registration lists against the city directory in one white precinct in order to determine the possibility of false registration. This did not prove feasible, but we came across a better process. We started checking the lists of residents in three large apartment complexes in one precinct against the new voter registration lists. Apartment houses, with their turnover in tenants, are particularly vulnerable to false voter registration.

We discovered enough discrepancies to confirm Mr. Hatcher's charges and asked the religious community to take direct action. Bishops, synodical officials, conference officers, and rabbis were asked to sign a telegram to the attorney general of the United States, urging him to take immediate action on Mr. Hatcher's campaign organization's request. I personally talked by telephone with John Doar, assistant attorney general for the Civil Rights Division of the Department of Justice. The call, set up by the Community Relations Service, requested him to recommend that the attorney general act promptly to insure a fair election and forestall violent reactions in the city.

Mr. Doar explained that the Department of Justice was reluctant to intervene in a local election, for the power exerted would be awesome and could determine the outcome of the vote. Nevertheless, he said that the telegram from high-level religious leaders, since it was nonpartisan, would be considered as the decision was debated. We sent the telegram. Religious leaders of all faiths and from both political parties participated.

Richard Hatcher filed a suit against the Lake County Election Board in United States District Court for the Northern District of Indiana, charging the board with violating federal laws by reducing Negro voting strength in the mayoral election. After twenty-two FBI agents checked the lists and investigated the inflated registration of voters in the First and Sixth Districts, the United States Department of Justice filed a suit against the Lake County Election Board under the 1965 Voting Rights Act and the Fourteenth Amendment to the Constitution. The suit was the first of its kind in the North.

In federal court, in Hammond, on Monday, November 6, a Democratic precinct committeewoman, Mrs. Marian Tokarski, testified for the government that she had, upon instruction, added fifty-one fictitious names to the voting rolls in her white precinct. As a result of this and other testimony, the court ordered a fair and nondiscriminatory election in compliance with the Constitution, the Civil Rights Act of 1960, the Voting Rights Act of 1965, and the election laws of the state of Indiana. The court order specified in detail the procedure to be followed to insure a fair election. When the polls opened the next morning, every election official of both parties received a copy of the court order, and copies were posted at each of the polling places by a United States marshal.

That night, when the votes were counted, Richard Hatcher won by a margin of 1,389 votes. He polled 39,330 votes to 37,941 for Mr. Radigan.

The federal government's intervention in the Lake County election in 1967 was absolutely essential, for the electoral process was being manipulated illegally in order to prevent a qualified black candidate from being elected to office. The church, without campaigning for either candidate, needed to exert its influence in support of just procedures and a fair election.

Richard Hatcher and Carl Stokes, who on the same date was elected in Cleveland, became the first black mayors in Northern cities. The elections of 1967 indicated that Black Power could utilize the political process in a nonviolent, nondestructive war that respected the democratic process.

These elections signaled that the votes of blacks and other minorities could not be exploited by white politicians in the future. Following his election Mr. Hatcher said, "Our victory was proof, if any was needed, that Negroes know how to make full use of the ballot box to make their wishes known."

Unfortunately, this use of Black Power was no more acceptable to large segments of the white community than revolutionary rhetoric and threats of violence. In Gary, a white-dominated county political organization sought to split the black community by appealing to the white backlash and using black extremism.

The Gary election was particularly important in alerting the white community to the reality of black unity and to the fact that the law protected Black Power when expressed through the electoral process. The election also demonstrated that there were white voting minorities ready to cast their ballots without regard to race when qualified candidates ran for office.

In addition, the election in Gary indicated to the religious community that there is a ministry to be performed when a political event leads to social crisis. The work of clergy and laity—Catholic, Jewish, and Protestant—was, for the most part, low profile, but it was brought to bear at strategic points and was a factor in averting violence through the support of a fair election.

The crisis team which emerged from the religious community played several roles. It not only helped locate white "ghost" voters, but it effected its own contingency plan as tension mounted in the city. Ministers, priests, and rabbis, assigned to key places in the community, monitored a variety of activities, maintained alternate lines of communication between critical points, mingled with crowds so that false rumors could be dispelled, and energetically helped maintain peace while vigorously promoting justice.

At one point, liaison between the black political organization and the ethnic neighborhoods rested heavily upon actions of the religious community. While the Democratic machine cranked out anxiety about the consequences of electing a black mayor, church representatives channeled accurate and reasonable information into the congregations, particularly in the Catholic ethnic parishes where surveys indicated that concern was most prevalent.

The work of the religious community in the Gary election was controversial, for in its pursuit of justice, it appeared partisan. Clergy met strong criticism by placing a half-page advertisement in the Gary *Post Tribune* on the Sunday immediately preceding the election. The simple ad was a "Voter's Prayer," written by

Rabbi Carl Miller of Temple Israel in Gary. It said, "Eternal God, give me the grace to avoid casting my ballot for black or white. Grant me rather the wisdom to choose on the basis of issues and qualifications." Many clergymen decided not to list their names underneath, fearing it would be interpreted, "Eternal God, enable me to vote black."

If a fraudulent election had proceeded in Gary in November, 1967, the repercussions would have been as serious as those which reverberated from Newark and Detroit four months previously. The election was vitally important. Voters cast their ballots for more than candidates. The election was a referendum on the viability of the democratic process and on the political opportunities of black citizenry.

4

Bombs in Jackson

Returning to Washington after the Gary election, I was assigned to a routine local church event, a "missional workshop" sponsored by the Commission on Missions of Galloway Memorial Methodist Church in Jackson, Mississippi, on November 17–18. I was to represent the Board of Christian Social Concerns.

Four years earlier in 1963, two bishops of the Methodist church had been refused admittance to a worship service at Galloway Church because one was white and the other black. The church ushers had linked arms to obstruct entrance. Since that time, the church had adopted an open-door policy. In the process of developing and applying the policy, six hundred members had withdrawn from the church, and thousands of dollars in pledges had been canceled. The church was in costly transition.

The workshop focused on "The Church in Mission" in order to point the church forward. More than fifty persons attended the two-day retreat at a Baptist camp near Jackson. A layman, Robert Kochtitzky, coordinated the effort.

The church's laity and clergy engaged in a highly sophisticated and fully informed series of discussions about the Christian congregation's witness in the social order. A number of precise, priority witness-points emerged in the city of Jackson, in the state of Mississippi, in the nation, and in the world. Avoiding safe generalities and worn banalities, the participants raised real and difficult problems and proposed resolute, demanding answers. It would require Christian faith to venture in the proposed directions.

For hours the members struggled to formulate strategies and tactics which would transform Galloway Methodist Church into a congregation in mission. They already knew some of the costs of witness exacted by their own community, but they prepared to carry on and assume even greater risks by the grace of the Lord.

The workshop ended, and the participants started home. I helped Bob Kochtitzky pack the blackboard, easel, projector, books, and other materials which he had brought to the retreat into his automobile. We then drove to his home at 1704 Poplar Street in Jackson where I was to be a guest that night. We planned to go to Sunday school and worship at Galloway Church the next day, Sunday, November 19. Then I would rent a car and drive up the state to visit projects of the Delta Ministry, sponsored by the National Council of Churches and supported by several major denominations.

Bob and I had arrived at his house about 9:00 P.M. His wife, Kay, served coffee in the living room as we chatted about the possible effects of the mission workshop. The conversation covered Milwaukee and Gary since they knew I had just come from assignments there and they were very interested in the church's ministries in both places. At eleven o'clock we started to bed, pausing at the bottom of the steps to talk over plans for the next day. I glanced into the dining room. Kay had set the table most attractively for breakfast the following morning.

My bedroom was comfortable, and I took my toothbrush and toothpaste into the adjoining bathroom. Kay and Bob were in their bedroom.

Five minutes later, at 11:05 P.M., a dynamite charge set on the front porch near the living room window detonated. Within seconds, flying wood, glass, and puffs of smoke and dust rolled through the rooms. The blast seemed to move the entire house.

The door of the bathroom crashed open. Lights flickered—went completely out—then flashed back on. I staggered momentarily, then heard the Kochtitzky's five-month-old son Christopher, crying in the background. Kay and Bob groped toward his crib, and I followed. A window had blown down beside the crib, but the glass missed the baby, and he was just frightened. No one was injured. Kay wrapped Christopher in a blanket, and we all proceeded downstairs, climbing over jagged pieces of lumber, stepping through plaster and glass. We crawled through a massive hole in the front of the house out onto the lawn. Chunks of the porch and pieces of the house lay in violently shaped patterns.

Neighbors ran over. Many had ostracized the Kochtitzkys because of their social involvements and friendships with Negroes. Now they clustered around in the semidarkness. One breathless man asked Bob, "What can we do? What can we do?"

Bob recognized him and said simply, "You can begin speaking up, man."

Police cars converged, breaking the darkness with flashing lights. Law enforcement officials and neighbors filled the front yard. Police surrounded the house, guarding any evidence until city detectives and FBI agents arrived.

Kay took the baby two blocks away to the home of Dr. and Mrs. T. W. Lewis. Bob and I sat in the back of a police cruiser, waiting for the bomb squad to arrive. The front of the house was heavily damaged. We shook as we recalled that only moments before we had been sitting directly in line with the explosion's main point of impact.

"Where was God in all of this?" we asked each other and agreed that the Holy Spirit may well have nudged us upstairs just moments ahead of the blast. Although God certainly did not cause the explosion, the Lord could well be seen through it.

The explosion had shaken all of us. Life waited to be lived again, a whole new world; yet the same old world was in need of the change discussed at the retreat. The bombing emphasized that need and pointed to the urgency. We both made some new commitments with our heads bowed and our hands trembling.

The bomb specialists arrived. Approaching the house, we could see the damage more clearly. The front porch was gone, the door blown to pieces, the windows broken and even the window frames dislodged. Inside the living room a large hole revealed where the charge had been set and the maximum force felt. The blast had smashed the furniture, blowing some of it across the room. The overstuffed sofa and chairs on which we had been sitting appeared raked by machine gun fire, riddled with fragments of concrete and wood. Pictures were slashed. Books were shredded on the shelves. A quiet home, immaculately clean and attractively decorated, had been violated.

Officers and agents rounded up some chairs and began questioning Bob and me. Bob described the events of the weekend and also related that on two successive nights sometime before, the doorbell of the Kochtitzky's home had rung, but no one was there when he answered. Several evenings that summer, he and Kay noticed two people sitting in a car across the strcet from their home. On one occasion, a cross was planted and burned in the backyard.

Bob explained his work with the Laymen's Overseas Service and described what he did as director of the Ecumenical Center for Renewal. He had to go over the word, *renewal* several times and interpret what it meant to his work with the church. I listened as Bob delineated the spiritual process by which congregations become alive witnesses so that social order can be constructively changed and personal lives altered. One effective renewal would be to prevent people from acting destructively and "causing this sort of thing to happen."

Sleep eluded us. Reporters came by. We secured the house after the police left. Finally, I went to another home, a couple of blocks away, but remained restless throughout the night. I presume that neither Kay nor Bob slept much either.

Although we missed the church school class, the next morning we were in a front pew at the worship service. It seemed the logical place to be.

The sermon topic printed in the bulletin, selected by the pastor Warren C. Hamby long before, was "Being Christian When It Is Not Easy." The pastor had rushed to the Kochtitzky's the night before when he was notified that two of his parishioners nearly had been killed. He kept vigil until the morning after the rest of us left.

In the pulpit Rev. Hamby raised his voice, "What had Mr.

Kochtitzky done to prompt this kind of violence? He had kept the integrity of Christian witness as a sensitive Christian in a society not yet willing for such a witness. He had taken seriously the convictions that were imparted to him by the teachings of the church school and the witness of the pulpit of this church. [Bob had attended Galloway Church since 1940.]

"He had dared to go beyond the respectable acquiescence of the polite forms of Christianity that so often characterize the poor witness of most of us. Who is to blame? Every pulpit where justice and mercy and goodwill have not been enough proclaimed; every alleged Christian who has thought more of his or her prejudices than of seeking the will of God and the spirit of Jesus Christ in attitude and behavior; every newspaper that has defended indefensible positions and voiced its own prejudices; the responsible elected officials of city and state who have been more concerned with expediency than integrity—here my friends, is the accumulated and collective guilt that is ours."

Following the service several laymen came directly to me and apologized for the bombing. As members of Galloway Methodist Church and as citizens of Jackson they wanted me to know how deeply they regretted the incident. I said that they need not apologize, for I had found violent resistance to social change every place. I recalled the drinking glasses dropped on us from hotel windows, stories above, as we marched on downtown Milwaukee sidewalks. Violence comes in different forms and at diverse points, but that is a national problem—not just one in a particular state or city.

The pastor was right, however. There is a collective responsibility, and lay persons spoke to that when they apologized to me; yet the responsibility includes all of us.

The experience that day with the people in Jackson, Mississippi, convinced me that the church cannot avoid violence in witnessing to a faith in Christ. We must not be violent, but we must not be intimidated by violence. We must confront the possibility of violence and even being its victims as we try to be faithful to a gospel which expresses profound love and insists upon justice.

5

Assassination in Memphis

After the disastrous summer months of 1967, following the 1965 and 1966 riots, could the rage and frustration which burst violently through the surface be mobilized into effective campaigns which would constructively affect the government and other institutions in society? The Milwaukee marches attempted this. Elections in Gary and Cleveland demonstrated that the political process could work at a local level even against great resistance.

The presidential address of Dr. Martin Luther King, Jr., to the 1967 annual Southern Christian Leadership Conference convention proposed a national strategy, utilizing massive civil disobedience and centering on the nation's capital. The Poor Peoples' Campaign, as it was later called, would gather up the latent rage, channel the deep despair, and provide a dramatic picture of the desperate needs of the poor. As Dr. King and his staff envisioned it, the Poor Peoples' Campaign would be a "constructive channel for responsive actions" to the Congress of the United States and within the departments of the federal government. The campaign was to be a biracial coalition of diverse groups. Poverty plagued more than just the black population even though the violence of hopelessness was most glaring in urban black ghettos.

In early 1968, Dr. King and Dr. Ralph David Abernathy, his

close associate, toured the country. They traveled thousands of miles, speaking to the poor in migrant farm labor camps, in the hollows of white Appalachia, on American Indian reservations, in Mexican American barrios, in black ghettos, and in Puerto Rican slums. Everywhere they invited community representatives to join them in Washington, D.C., to pledge nonviolence, and to bring their poverty needs with them.

Typically, Dr. King would say, as he remarked in Albany, Georgia, on February 21, "We are going to start a movement. And we're not going to Washington just for one day. No . . . no, we are going in a wait-in and stay-in movement. Come young and old, come sick and well, come to Washington. We are going to build a shanty town in Washington . . . and we're going to let the whole world know what it means to be poverty-stricken."

Three thousand persons were to be selected from ten different cities and several rural areas across the entire nation to live in a shanty town which would be patterned after the veterans' bonus marches of the 1930s.

Obviously the Poor Peoples' Campaign would not be another euphoric 1963 march on Washington. The planning combined a nationally scaled 1955 Montgomery bus boycott and a Birmingham demonstration at the seat of the federal government. Caravans of poor, originating in every part of the country and coming from every direction, would multiply the Selma to Montgomery march several times.

Dr. King hoped that large numbers of white persons again would join the ranks of the movement, identify with the poor, and help furnish the political leverage necessary to move the federal government so that nonviolent and constructive alternatives to the riots could be developed before summer, 1968.

Dr. King not only knew that the torch of despair had been passed from ghetto to ghetto in the summer of 1967, but also that the response of the white population was a prelude to severe repression. Whites were arming themselves. A climate nurturing retaliatory governmental violence was developing. Pressures for clamping the lid back onto the well of grievances among the poor were growing.

The line between a rigid repressive society and a compassionate responsive one was being drawn. Some mechanism had to be offered to allow the country to pull back from violence—white and black—and to consider serious alternatives. The Poor Peoples' Campaign was meant to be that mechanism.

No one wanted the poor to come to Washington in 1968, except the Southern Christian Leadership Conference. The liberal Northern press and other communications media, so vocal in exposing the discrimination of the South to the eyes of the nation, shunned the proposed Poor Peoples' Campaign. Other civil rights sponsors of the 1963 march on Washington were disinterested. Some called it "old-fashioned"; others saw it as dangerous.

Bayard Rustin, coordinator of the 1963 march, tried to persuade Dr. King in Atlanta to cancel plans for the campaign. Having failed, he returned to New York, saying, "Dr. King is sincere in believing there is a terrible urgency and that if Congress does not act, the nation will be faced with more riots."

For the most part the churches nationally were silent when Dr. King called for support. In February I attended some of the meetings between SCLC staff and national denominational staff. I received the impression from the long discussions that the churches would make little commitment to such a controversial project. Church representatives also seemed to believe that the intended nonviolent campaign could generate rioting, not only in the national capital, but in other cities.

The real danger, as I saw it then, was the isolation of the Southern Christian Leadership Conference from the kind of support essential to keep the campaign nonviolent while aggressively pursuing its objectives. After a meeting with SCLC staff, I proposed that an office of liaison sponsored by the National Council of Churches be established. Each national denomination would furnish some staff for short-term assignments and others for the entire campaign. The office of liaison would channel accurate information about the campaign to the churches. It would also locate resources, including money, supportive of the nonviolent strategy and the political objectives of the campaign, produce materials which would interpret the campaign to the church constituency, and maintain lines of communication with all parts of the government in case of critical developments. Finally, the office would identify with the campaign on a daily basis to forestall tactical isolation of SCLC and the participating poor.

The National Council of Churches in New York, approving the proposal, requested that I be the director of the National Council of Churches Office of Liaison for the Poor Peoples' Campaign. For six months, I would be in the campaign full time.

The SCLC staff welcomed the liaison operation being set up in Washington. They channeled information directly to us and used the new office opened in the Methodist Building on Capitol Hill as a coordinated point of contact with the several denominations. They were uncertain, of course, as to what support the Office of Liaison represented, and admittedly, we were unsure about the realities of our role. We could not make any commitments on behalf of the churches, but the Office of Liaison was a mechanism *through* which commitments could be made and through which resources could be brokered.

Criticism of the campaign continued to mount during March, 1968. The April edition of the *Reader's Digest*, circulated after the middle of the month, contained an article entitled, "Martin Luther King's March on Washington," which asserted, "One thing is certain: whether or not all of the protestor's plans materialize, the nation faces international humiliation as a result of the Washington campaign. Communism's worldwide propaganda apparatus is set for a field day. Communist-bloc newsmen will cable home Washington-dateline dispatches on the 'starvation' and 'misery' of 'oppressed Americans.' Powerful transmitters will beam the distorted accounts to Africa, Asia, and Latin America. 'If this demonstration gets out of hand,' said Stefan Possony, one of the country's top experts on psychological warfare, 'if there is any violence at all, the damage to our prestige would be incalculable.' "

The author of the article disregarded the 1967 riots. By that time the National Advisory Commission on Civil Disorders, named by President Johnson, had concluded that the riots were not attempts to subvert the social order of the United States.

"Instead," the report said, "most of those who attacked white authority and property seemed to be demanding fuller participation in the social order and the material benefits enjoyed by the vast majority of American citizens."

The author of the *Reader's Digest* article appeared to express a greater concern for the prestige of the United States than for the problems of the poor and the presage of violence tied to those problems.

Before it was possible for the Communist-bloc newsmen to cable home the dispatches which would "humiliate" the United States, thirteen hundred garbage workers went on strike in Memphis, Tennessee, attempting to gain recognition for their union. The city government reacted with bludgeoning police power, and the black community retaliated with a boycott of downtown stores. The stand-off evoked an immediate prospect of violence. Dr. King and other SCLC staff persons were asked to devise nonviolent strategies of support for the sanitation workers.

Recognizing that Memphis represented precisely the kind of issue which had to be faced if the Poor Peoples' Campaign was to be effective in Washington, Dr. King joined the Memphis protest. He attempted to keep his heavy commitments elsewhere and to continue the campaign planning, but Memphis took more and more of his time. There was no pulling out either, for that would discredit the SCLC at the very time it needed all its strength.

Then came the crisis. Some black teenagers broke the line of march led by Dr. King and smashed windows of downtown stores. Demands for the cancellation of the Poor Peoples' Campaign increased; the threat of violence in Washington seemed real now.

Immediately after the disruption in Memphis, Dr. King preached at the National Cathedral in Washington. In his sermon on Sunday, March 31, once more he interpreted the necessity for the Poor Peoples' Campaign and its objectives. He found it difficult to persuade even his friends that nonviolence could work in the nation's capital.

Wedged between warnings from Washington and threats in Memphis, on Wednesday evening, he spoke at a rally supporting the garbage workers: "And then I got into Memphis. And some began to say the threats, or to talk about the threats that were out. What would happen to me from some of our sick white brothers. Well, I don't know what will happen now. We've got some difficult days ahead. But it doesn't really matter to me now. Because I've been to the mountain top . . . and I've looked over. And I've seen the promised land. I may not get there with you. But I want you to know tonight, that we, as a people, will get to the promised land. And so I'm happy tonight. I'm not worried about anything. I'm not fearing any man. 'Mine eyes have seen the glory of the coming of the Lord.' "

The next evening, April 4, 1968, Dr. Martin Luther King, Jr., was standing outside room 306 on the balcony of the Lorraine Motel, 406 Mulberry Street, in Memphis. A rifle fired from the back of a shabby, low-cost rooming house at 418½ South Main Street, just opposite the motel, shattered Dr. King's jaw, ripped his throat, and severed his spinal column. He died instantly at 6:01 P.M.

6

Poor People's Campaign in Washington, D.C.

Hours after the death of Dr. Martin Luther King, Jr., a hundred cities in the United States began to burn. In Washington, D.C., the government lowered its flags to half-mast in respect for the person whose leadership it had been rejecting, one of three times in the history of the United States that the federal flag had flown at half-mast for a civilian other than when a president or other high federal official died.

The president of the United States, the vice-president, the chief justice, and the associate justices of the Supreme Court, the majority and minority leaders of both houses of Congress, and notables from throughout the city came to the memorial service at Washington Cathedral the morning of April 5. Deep respect and profound appreciation for the life of Martin Luther King, Jr., was expressed from the very pulpit where four days earlier he had preached in defense of the Poor Peoples' Campaign.

By the time the worship service was dismissed, chaos had broken loose in large parts of the city. Business buildings and houses were aflame. Two blocks from the White House, groups of black teenagers hit and looted the stores. Employees were dismissed from federal offices and many businesses; the streets were choked with traffic, and panic was written on drivers' faces.

As I made my way from Washington Cathedral back to my

office, I watched the city empty of suburban whites as rage and violence poured across it. Thick black clouds of smoke hung over everything, and as I walked toward the Hill, the Capitol itself was blotted from view. The most extensive burning within the capital since the British invaded it in 1813 was taking place.

I fought against the tide. Police cars and emergency vehicles struggled to get to assignments. Sirens screamed from every direction, but when they paused, a strange quietness accompanied the rapid and radical change.

Uniforms outnumbered civilian dress as troops were authorized and organized. Military vehicles replaced the cars that had fled the city. Protection arrived for government buildings, and on the steps of the Capitol, airborne troops stood with machine guns ready to fire.

Fires raged and spread; a curfew was announced and enforced. Several of us stayed throughout the night in the United Methodist Building on Capitol Hill. We watched and we waited—and we prayed. Forces were firm but not punitive. Anger drained away, and those who had tried to use the time of violence disappeared. Instantly the city created an emergency office to expedite the flow of supplies to those who had been caught in the destruction. The situation began to ease.

Actually, Mrs. Martin Luther King, Jr., Dr. Ralph David Abernathy—the King family and the staff of the Southern Christian Leadership Conference—led our nation through the dark days which followed the assassination. Mrs. King appeared on television and, with poise, appealed for an end to the violence which had erupted, saying that her husband would have been grieved about such a reaction to his death.

The King family and the SCLC staff joined in rapidly planning a funeral which would dramatize the message of Dr. King's life. It was to be a great celebration of faith for the nation and a service of rededication for those who would struggle nonviolently for social justice.

On the day before the funeral, when Dr. King was scheduled to have marched in Memphis, Mrs. King and her children walked with Dr. Abernathy, Rev. Andrew Young, Rev. James Lawson, and thousands of others, demonstrating support for the garbage workers. Dr. King's work was going forward!

The staff of SCLC announced that the Poor Peoples' Campaign would continue. Even though planning was seriously behind schedule, every effort was made to recruit the poor, plan the caravans, arrange for the establishment of a shanty town, and prepare proposals for various departments of government.

When we received word in the Office of Liaison that the Poor Peoples' Campaign was to proceed, we rapidly communicated with the NCC in New York. The liaison office which had been minimally activated during March became almost instantaneously fully operational.

Caravans of poor were being organized from seven different points of origin. SCLC was concerned about the problems the caravans might face in obtaining housing and food and in dealing with a succession of law enforcement agencies. We called for national denominational staff persons to drop their work and come to Washington to be briefed and then assigned in rotation to the caravans. Some staff were to move ahead of the contingents of poor, negotiating for lodging, arranging for free meals, consulting with police, and keeping in direct contact with the liaison office.

In most instances, cities were hospitable to the caravans. They made public parks available for camping and opened city buildings for lodging; businesses offered food and supplies. Church councils and other religious organizations brokered the services and offered the use of their buildings and equipment as the caravans passed through. Our staff reported that in some instances the assistance given to caravans seemed to be based more on making sure that the caravans promptly left the town or city than in offering them any help in taking their grievances to Washington, D.C.

Caravans of poor were officially launched from the balcony of the Lorraine Motel in Memphis, on May 2, 1968. Thousands gathered below in the parking lot of the motel and on Mulberry Street for the ceremony. On that day, Dr. Ralph Abernathy, Mrs. Coretta Scott King, and SCLC leadership dedicated a marble memorial plaque placed on the wall outside room 306.

Late the preceding evening I was called to room 306. Dr. Abernathy showed me the marble marker which was to be set the following morning. He gave me the list of persons who would participate in the service of memorial and dedication and then asked me to write the ceremony. I was to have it ready for distribution by 10:00 A.M. the next day. Returning to my room, I opened a Gideon Bible and started to work. Early the next day I took the copy to Dr. Abernathy for his approval and went to the First Methodist Church. Within an hour and a half, the staff mimeographed and collated enough copies for distribution to the assembled crowd.

When the caravan left Memphis, I went down to Marks, Mississippi, a town which SCLC describes as the last place where Dr. King was known to have cried. He had wept there in January as he saw the desperation and yet the courage of the impoverished black population. Traveling dirt back roads and visiting families in dilapidated houses, I saw for myself some of the needs driving people toward Washington. In one shack I visited with a mother sick in bed—the only bed in the place. Five scantily dressed children, ages five through twelve, clustered around. I could see plainly that they were hungry—really hungry and so was their mother. When the children took me out into a back room, presumably the kitchen, I opened a battered, inoperative electric refrigerator (they had no electricity) and found only a small bag of flour and two shriveled apples. I brought in the food I had in the car and gave it to the mother to share. I couldn't do case work here; I didn't know the facts. But there was sickness and conspicuous hunger.

In another house, and it is generous to call the structure a "house," I found equally desperate conditions. Two older black women, unable to afford food stamps, had asked a neighbor man to butcher their goat, which had been a source of milk. They needed the food. I saw the fly-covered carcass of the skinny animal hanging by a rope on the little porch. They wouldn't get much meat from it—and then what?

The poverty about which Dr. King had spoken was real. Hunger actually existed in America. He knew that it was mainly hidden and silent but that it stretched across the land and made life a survival exercise for millions of persons of all races in rural areas and in cities.

The Poor Peoples' Campaign was designed to translate the distress and despair into positive recommendations to the government. It was not intended to be a highly organized, finely polished lobbying effort. It was meant to be a campaign in which real and bona fide poor persons, with the sponsorship of SCLC and the help of others, would have an opportunity to speak for themselves with government officials who made the decisions which influenced the lives of the poor.

From the beginning, I believed the campaign might be more of an inconvenience than a threat. The poor were somewhat impatient and demanding; yet they were basically courteous and respectful. I thought the campaign had a chance to evoke some responses and arouse some consciences if the public would support it.

Unfortunately, plans for the campaign never caught up with events after the Memphis strike and Dr. King's assassination. Serious problems developed as soon as Resurrection City, the shanty town, was opened. Delays in the deliveries of materials joined with bad weather to insure the city would not be ready when the caravans arrived.

Resurrection City USA, even when constructed, became filled with confusion, disorganization, and some violence. Everything seemed to work against the campaign, but the weather most of all. There was more rain in Washington, D.C., in May and June of 1968 than had been reported for those months since 1908.

Eventually Resurrection City literally sank into the mud, and the plywood shanties began to float in what appeared to be an annex to the Reflecting Pool. People lost their boots and shoes trying to walk through the city; the mud literally sucked them right off people's feet.

In the media the mud got more attention than the carefully drawn proposals to the government which had been prepared for the Poor Peoples' Campaign by the Washington Research Center. Some believed the poor living in the mud on the Mall desecrated the capital.

When Resurrection City construction began, the Church of the

Brethren brought several volunteers to Washington to help construct the plywood shanties. We requested a shanty for the National Council of Churches which could serve as a small liaison center and also as a place where staff could live on a rotating basis.

In addition, the Methodist Building became a place where leaders of the several minority groups who were participating in the campaign would meet to coordinate plans. The weather wiped out the meeting places in Resurrection City.

Conducting the prolonged protest was demanding work for SCLC leadership and for the contingents of poor. They were simultaneously attempting to lobby in the Congress, negotiate with high officials of several federal departments, utilize the media to educate the public nationally, maintain a nonviolent commitment among a variety of groups, and simply survive. They had come to Washington to make demands upon the government, but they made greater demands upon themselves. It was not easy work.

And they were exposed to constant scrutiny. More seemed to be expected from the poor than from the government. One of the criticisms was that the poor did not properly behave themselves in Washington. Rev. Andrew Young, executive vice-president of SCLC, replied: "When we invited the poor to come to Washington, we did not ask only the stable poor, the healthy poor, the secure poor, or the respectable poor. We asked the *poor* to come, and we asked only that they participate nonviolently. What we have is a slice of poverty placed under a microscope."

White support for the campaign never really developed, certainly not sufficiently to bring any real pressure to bear on Congress. It just did not seem possible to convert the fear of whites which ran rampant during 1967 riots into assistance for a nonviolent appeal for alternate solutions to the crisis. Law and order was rapidly becoming governmental policy and receiving widespread white support.

Soon the government which had, out of respect for Dr. Martin Luther King, Jr., endured the Poor Peoples' Campaign and tolerated Resurrection City, determined that the campaign must come to a conclusion. The national political campaigns of 1968 were beginning, and a Poor Peoples' Campaign should not continue in the midst of the political conventions which were scheduled in Miami Beach and Chicago in July and August. On June 21, the government announced that the permit which had been granted for the use of the Mall would be revoked. The deadline set for leaving the area and dismantling Resurrection City was 10:00 A.M., June 24.

Several of us were called to Dr. Abernathy's shanty late on Sunday night to plan the closing of the city and to arrange transportation for the poor out of Washington, D.C. I took James Hamilton, director of the Washington office of the National Council of Churches, with me. We spent nearly the entire night huddled together in the small plywood structure figuring out what to do. Top SCLC leadership discussed at length the problems of dismantling Resurrection City nonviolently. Many living in the city said they would not leave peaceably because the federal government had not really made an effective response to their appeals. It was obvious by midmorning of the next day that the city would be cleared by police; so SCLC leaders decided to organize one last protest demonstration and to march to the Capitol to present a final petition to Congress. They expected to confront police. Attempts were made to negotiate with the Metropolitan Police Department of the District of Columbia, the United States Department of Justice, and the United States Park Police.

Throughout the night we were in contact with the government, considering alternatives. At 4:00 A.M., SCLC strategy was finalized, and the meeting broke up. We were to meet again for a press conference at the front gate of Resurrection City at 7:00 A.M. As I left, ready to step back out into the continuing rain, Dr. Abernathy said, "You will be with me at 7:00 A.M., won't you? You'll stay with me, won't you?"

I had assumed that I would go home, sleep three hours, and then monitor the protest march as it moved from the lower Mall toward the Capitol. Dr. Abernathy was asking me to participate in the march and to help move the people up toward Capitol Hill. He knew that the police working around Resurrection City had become aggressive and had provoked some confrontations with the residents. Since there weren't many white persons around at that point, I assumed that he wanted a clergyman, who was also white, to fill in the front ranks with an interracial image. The strategy had worked in other places.

I told him I'd be back at 7:00 A.M. With Jim Hamilton, I drove to my home in northwest Washington, and we sat at the dining room table, discussing how I could participate in the march—possibly be arrested—since I was semiofficially representing the National Council of Churches. On the other hand, we knew how important it was for the demonstration to be nonviolent and for Resurrection City to be cleared prior to any police action. We agreed that I should be there, but that as soon as I knew what was really going to happen, I would check with Dr. Charles Spivey, director of the Department of Social Justice of the National Council of Churches in New York.

I went to the press conference. Dr. Abernathy announced the final demonstration and then waded through the mud, calling people out of the shanties, tapping on the roofs of the little huts, asking the poor to gather up their few belongings and come with him to the Capitol to deliver one last message and to be arrested if necessary. At first, only a few came out. It was early; yet all around police were assembling. Fifteen hundred police in riot gear were ready to move in.

Having circled through the city once, Dr. Abernathy noticed that only twenty or thirty persons were ready to go with him. Police and media representatives watched closely. It looked bad. Dr. Abernathy decided to walk through again, and I walked at his side. This time, however, the people started turning out of the shanties; they came from every direction. Some carried their few possessions in shopping bags or brown paper sacks; others simply left their belongings. Picking up the pace, they fell in behind Dr. Abernathy and his aides. The march was on.

The group decided to go to the Department of Agriculture Building on the way to the Capitol to give one last word to the secretary of agriculture about the food stamp needs of the poor. When we arrived, we selected five persons to go inside and deliver the message. Officials allowed us into the building and escorted us to an office where an assistant to the secretary met us. I stepped out of that meeting a moment, to a secretarial desk, to call Dr. Spivey in New York. By then, I knew we would be arrested. The protest on the Capitol grounds would violate a federal statute. I couldn't reach Dr. Spivey at home or at his office. He was enroute to the Interchurch Center. The next best thing, I thought, was to call Dr. Dudley Ward, general secretary of the Board of Church and Society (then Christian Social Concerns), my superior. He answered his office telephone. "Dr. Ward," I said, "I am at the Department of Agriculture with Dr. Abernathy and the group from the Poor Peoples' Campaign. We are marching toward the Capitol, and I think we are going to be arrested. Can you tell me what the policy is on staff being arrested?"

"I will check on that," Dr. Ward said. "Where will you be?"

"We'll be at Constitution Avenue and First Street, N.W., in about twenty or twenty-five minutes."

"I'll get back to you there," he said.

We marched on toward the point of expected confrontation. As we came across the Mall and headed toward the corner where we knew we would be met by police, we could see at a distance a very large crowd. It was at least as large as the group of protestors marching with us. As we got nearer, we saw that the sidewalks and part of the street were filled with police and television and newspaper reporters, as well as many onlookers.

We tried to maneuver into place, but we could barely squeeze onto the sidewalks. (Later we were arrested for blocking that sidewalk, but it was blocked before we arrived.) We crowded onto it at a particular place as we were directed to do by the police. Then we waited. The police lined up opposite us, one or two feet away, and held their riot sticks horizontally at chest level while we negotiated.

I could see arrest coming, but I still did not have official approval for being arrested. It was particularly important for me to be representing the church at this time. I watched the whole crowd carefully, looking for Dr. Ward. Finally I saw his head bobbing up and down as he was obviously jumping up slightly every moment or so. He spotted me and pressed through the mass of people, weaving in and out, until he came right up to me. He then advised me, "I called Bishop Golden in San Francisco and Bishop Thomas in Des Moines [they were officers of our board], and they have given you permission to be arrested." Just in time! Within five minutes, I was arrested, next after Dr. Abernathy.

Bussed to a police substation, we were formally booked and our personal possessions taken from us—a routine practice. It means giving up your watch, money, and so on.

Then we were crowded into small cells where we waited for transportation to the District of Columbia jail. After being taken there, we were kept up until 5:30 A.M. as they processed us—mug shots, fingerprints, delousing, and showers. They took our clothes, and for some hours, we stood naked in crowded quarters, waiting to move through each step of the process.

We were allowed to sleep about an hour (I couldn't), served breakfast outside the cells, and then transported to the district court house. In the van into which I was placed, were some prisoners who had been arrested on charges other than those related to the demonstration the day before. I was handcuffed to a man who told me he was a suspect in a robbery.

When we arrived at the court house, we had to wait in the van for a while but then were escorted into the "tank"—a holding cell for prisoners awaiting arraignment. While we waited, we stretched out on the floor. Some of us had not slept for nearly forty-eight hours, and in our fatigue, I suspect we looked like drunks who had been picked up on Thirteenth Street the night before.

The Southern Christian Leadership Conference with its philosophy of nonviolent social action and civil disobedience had a policy of "jail—no bail." If one disobeyed the laws, he or she accepted the penalties. When lawyers from the NAACP Legal Defense came to the tank, they advised everyone to plead *nolo contendere* or "no contest," with two exceptions. Hosea Williams, who had been arrested in Resurrection City when he had stayed there with some other SCLC staff persons to counterbalance the presumed violently inclined group who had refused to march out, was one of them. I was the other. Dr. Abernathy came to me in the tank and said that I had been selected as the "lamb" to be bailed out, to plead not guilty, and to be tried on the charges. SCLC hoped that I would be exonerated and that we could obtain a decision that the federal statute barring demonstrations on Capitol grounds was unconstitutional.

Later that morning, while persons were being sentenced as much as ninety days for the crime of blocking the sidewalks or disorderly conduct, arrangements were made for me to be released on a bond. Since I had no money, the lawyer obtained it for me, took me to the office of the clerk of the court, and processed the paper work. He left before I was finally released, believing that everything was set. When I was let go, I did not have a dime to call the office. I certainly had no bus fare or money for a taxi; so I walked the several blocks to the Methodist Building. People stared at me—a disheveled man in a clerical collar, splattered with mud, wrinkled clothing, mussed hair, and uncertain step.

While Dr. Abernathy was in jail, his staff sought to recruit clergy and other persons who would come to Washington, D.C., and be arrested, if necessary, to witness for the cause of the poor. Using Dr. King's "Letter from a Birmingham Jail" as a model, Dr. Abernathy wrote a letter, "From a Jail in America," addressed to "My dear fellow clergymen: I stand guilty of defending the poor, and I cheerfully accept the penalty . . . and today I ask you to join us."

It was Dr. Abernathy's twentieth time in jail. Very few persons responded to his call. The tide was running out for the campaign.

As might have been expected, it was said that the Poor Peoples' Campaign failed because it was not led by Dr. King. What was lacking, it was implied, was Dr. King's eloquence, his charisma, and his genius for timing. Dr. King was missed—more by Dr. Abernathy than by anyone else, I am sure. Yet the Poor Peoples' Campaign would have failed, to the degree that it did, even if Dr. King had been present. Clear signs of that preceded his death.

The failures of the Poor Peoples' Campaign lay in more than the weather, of course, and in even more than Dr. King's death.

Nineteen sixty-eight was the year of gigantic political shifts. Four days before Dr. King's assassination in Memphis, President Johnson announced that he would not be a candidate for reelection the next November. The Tet offensive in Vietnam had wiped out a strategy for a peace to be won by arms, and in the United States the antiwar movement became confirmed as a legitimate object of middle-class and middle-aged support. Without any design, the campaign to end the war took the place of the campaign to end poverty. To Dr. King and others, the goals were consistent, for the national resources which were being expended in Vietnam reduced those desperately needed at home. The poor in Vietnam were being killed with money required to help the poor in the United States.

Nevertheless, the movements competed for energy, money, time, media attention, and volunteers. Gradually, as the peace movement became more respectable, support shifted from the old civil rights and antipoverty forces. These causes would be tabled for the time being.

At that time, I wrote that the Poor Peoples' Campaign failed because the poor always fail—because they are powerless. Yet in the spring and early summer of 1968, a president resigned and a nonviolent leader was assassinated, as was Senator Robert F. Kennedy, who publicly had supported the Poor Peoples' Campaign and symbolized the hope of the poor among the several possible candidates for the presidency. Ironically, Senator Kennedy's death, coupled with the impact of the death of Dr. King, gave impetus to the "law and order" political crusade which was ultimately victorious.

In spite of all the fears, the Poor Peoples' Campaign was not violent. Dr. King, in planning for the campaign, said that although the campaign would be resisted, it would reduce the possibility of riots in the summer of 1968. It did.

The real purpose of the campaign was to create social change. Although not much public support or congressional action moved in that direction, there were social change forces released in the summer of 1968.

The Poor Peoples' Campaign probably gave this country some

additional time—time which the poor could not afford but which the society in shock urgently needed. However, the campaign also insured that the groups which came then with their nonviolent appeal would some day return. We are now using the time they gave us.

After Resurrection City, USA, had been destroyed by the government, a National Park Service employee was heard saying to a tourist as he pointed toward the area where the resodding had begun, "In two or three months you will never know there had been a Resurrection City." When you look at the Mall now, you cannot tell that the poor camped there in 1968. When you walk there, you realize that the grass is growing beneath our feet.

My trial was held in the summer of 1968. I was sobered when I saw on the docket, "The United States versus John P. Adams." I was charged only with disorderly conduct, for having blocked a sidewalk. Mine was a test case for the other 318 persons arrested at the Capitol. I was found guilty, fined twenty-five dollars, and given a suspended sentence. The Washington *Evening Star* said that the highlight of the trial was the appearance of Rev. Ralph David Abernathy who testified that the campaigners were going to the Capitol to present a statement on the needs of the poor. The article also said, "During a brief recess in the trial, a group from the Poor Peoples' Campaign gave Adams a set of cuff links and sang 'Happy Birthday.' "

Dr. Abernathy had had an SCLC staff person purchase them that morning. They were black onyx with gold setting. I remember the day as a happy birthday and one on which my convictions were strengthened.

The lawyers representing me appealed the conviction, and thirteen months later, it was overturned in the D.C. Court of Appeals. The court ruled that since the government had not claimed that we were in breach of peace, we could not be convicted for unlawful assembly in the incommoding of a sidewalk.

The next month I was in Chicago for the 1968 Democratic National Convention, riding on the first wagon of the Poor Peoples' Campaign mule train which took the needs of the nation's poor to the Democrats. Dr. Abernathy drove the first wagon, followed by five others, down South Michigan Avenue and brought the train to a halt in front of the Conrad Hilton Hotel. Deputy Superintendent James Rochford, now superintendent of police for the city of Chicago, came to the lead wagon and said, "Dr. Abernathy, I need this street badly. Can you give it to us? What are your plans?"

Courteously, Dr. Abernathy said, "I was going to have a press conference here and then move on."

Rochford then suggested, "I will have a cruiser escort you over into Grant Park, and you can have your press conference there. You can pull the wagons right up onto the lawn."

Dr. Abernathy agreed and signaled the mules to move. We went across the street and over the curb, but when the wagon hit the curb, I popped right off since I was not holding on securely. Three SCLC mule skinners picked me up from the sidewalk and put me back on the wagon. The antiwar movement supporters, gathered around for the press conference, cheered Dr. Abernathy and the SCLC. The poor peoples' demands were read. We moved out of the park.

Later that day, I watched the confrontation between the police and some of the antiwar groups. What I saw in 1968 took me to Miami Beach in 1972, determined to do everything possible to prevent a repetition of what the Walker Report had called "a police riot." Riot or not, it was a bloody confrontation between predominantly white, middle-class young people who sought an end to the war in Vietnam and the Chicago police whose extra-legal and violence-prone control measures had been fully sanctioned by the powerful Mayor Daly. As Andy Young said to me at the time, "Now that white youth have also experienced this, a radical change will come."

The change came, but not until after Kent State.

7

The Black Manifesto

In 1969, the Black Manifesto was delivered to the predominantly white churches of America. It came at a time when the churches essentially had withdrawn support from nonviolent social change. Just two weeks before the Black Manifesto was first taken to the interdenominational Riverside Church on Morningside Heights in Manhattan, Dr. Ralph Abernathy had said: "At a time when nonviolence is facing its greatest test, as it directly confronts the violent alternatives, the church has largely retreated. When the riots came, religious support began to slip. Apparently religious leaders did not want to run the risks that nonviolence has to run when it gives leadership in a violent time."

The Black Manifesto reflected the impatience and the discouragement felt by those parts of the black community which refused to accept the faltering concern of the white churches as the black community shifted its attention from civil rights to a demand for economic justice.

In May, 1969, the words *Black Power*, which had been shouted on a highway in Mississippi in 1966, chanted in the streets in 1967, and shaped to the Poor Peoples' Campaign out of respect to Dr. King in 1968, were suddenly and raucously amplified into the churches through the Black Manifesto.

Previously, the predominantly white churches had been able to avoid the implications of Black Power, for the words seemed to be directed toward government and toward other social institutions. There was no missing the point of the Black Manifesto: The words were intended for the churches as well. The churches, for the most part, had stepped back from those who shouted Black Power. In the minds of too many whites the words seemed synonymous with violence. Since violence could not be condoned, Black Power was little understood and minimally supported. The Black Manifesto changed all of that.

The Black Manifesto emerged from a National Black Economic Development Conference, held in Detroit, Michigan, April 25–27, 1969. The conference, attended by more than five hundred black persons, came to a turning point when James Forman presented a document indicting a white racist system which perpetuated historic injustices, subtly sanctioned by the religious community. The document, the Black Manifesto, demanded reparations of five hundred million dollars from white Christian churches and Jewish synagogues for use in establishing a black-controlled land bank, publishing companies, radio and television networks, a center to research the problems of black people, a community organization training center, a National Black Labor Strike and Defense Fund, and an International Black Appeal.

Now the demands were not being made of the government; they were being made of the churches. Now the appeal was not phrased in Christian theological language, as had been the "Letter from a Birmingham Jail." The introduction to the Black Manifesto was framed in Marxist terms. Now there was no assurance of nonviolence. The manifesto suggested the necessity for the use of force and the power of the gun.

The Black Manifesto instructed delegates and members of the Black Economic Development Conference to stage sit-in demonstrations at selected black and white churches and to make "quick use of the press" in order to "heighten the tension" and win the demands in a short time.

On May 4, 1969, exactly one year before the killing of students at Kent State University, Mr. Forman, former national chairman of the Student Non-Violent Coordinating Committee (SNCC), militantly marched up the center aisle of the interdenominational Riverside Church, interrupted a service of Holy Communion, and began inflicting upon the churches the charges and demands of the Black Manifesto. Immediately, the tension was heightened, not only in Riverside Church, but in the Interchurch Center, which stands less than a hundred yards away and houses the offices of the National Council of Churches and the agency headquarter offices of several major Protestant denominations. Riverside Church was given one week to meet four demands which had been tailored to that particular congregation: (1) Give to BEDC 60 percent of the church's annual income from investments; (2) furnish a list of all church assets and negotiate a percentage of these to BEDC; (3) make available free office space and unrestricted telephone use; (4) allow unrestricted use of the church's radio station. Riverside Church did not respond directly to BEDC. Instead, the board of deacons voted a fixed percentage of the annual budget to be set aside for projects for all disadvantaged people. The church received from the courts a civil restraining order that would place in contempt any individual who interfered with a worship service or any other church activity. In essence, the church recognized what it called "the needs behind the demands" of BEDC, but it opposed the disruptive tactics, and it rejected BEDC as a direct recipient of church funds. However, the senior minister, Dr. Ernest Campbell, both in sermons and statements, furnished a theological confirmation of the concept of reparations, substantiated the magnitude of the injustices described in the Black Manifesto, and challenged the churches to share their resources with those whom the BEDC had called "the exploited and colonized subjects in the United States."

James Forman burned the restraining order when it was presented to him. The spark jumped to the Interchurch Center, and in rapid fire the national offices of several denominations were confronted with escalated demands—50 million dollars, 60 million dollars, 130 million dollars, 200 million dollars, percentages of profits from investments, and donations of land and buildings. The Black Economic Development Conference was deadly serious, and as Mr. Forman said, "We are pursuing our demands for reparations in peace, but we are psychologically prepared to run the money-lenders, hustlers, crooks, investment brokers, and racists out of the temples and churches as Jesus did."

Confrontations with denominations included the occupation of offices, the use of "liberated" equipment, the nearly total disruption of agency work, a sympathy strike by employees, and a serious polarization between a large number of white and black staff members.

After some days of disruption, the Board of Trustees of the Interchurch Center, the National Council of Churches, and seven church agencies, representing four national denominations which were tenants in the center, obtained a restraining order in the New York Supreme Court. The order barred James Forman and his associates from entering or remaining in the offices of the center without permission, and it enjoined him from employing force or violence or the threat of force or violence against the property or the employees of the center. The restraining order flashed like a flare within the Interchurch Center. Mr. Forman replied, "If the racist Christians have gotten an injunction, let them enforce it, for I shall stay." And then he hurled the challenge, "We call upon all those so-called brave Christians who were so eager to march in Mississippi and Selma to come immediately to 475 Riverside Drive and interpose their bodies between the racist New York police and us."

Now, within the Interchurch Center, every working relationship became strained. Every corner of the building was a pocket of fear. Events seem to crash down one upon another, and the inevitability of violence, desired by no one, seemed expected by almost everyone.

On June 17, the day on which the injunction was obtained, I was invited to New York as part of a crisis team being formed by the Women's Division of the Board of Global Ministries of the United Methodist Church. We rapidly set up an office a few blocks from the Interchurch Center, installed additional telephones, and recruited several persons of various denominations, both black and white. We hoped our operation could reduce the possibility of violence and assist in opening and maintaining every possible line of communication between those who were originally in confrontation, as well as among the several serious factions which had developed as the conflict continued.

Church executives, denominational officials, caucus representatives, and BEDC spokesmen were in and out of a variety of meetings which extended through the working hours and often long into the night. We kept in contact with persons in every meeting so that we would have accurate information about each of the positions and be able to anticipate some of the problems that might develop as the positions were asserted. Not only did we keep a live and ready file of all materials which were being published, distributed, and exchanged, but we analyzed them so that we, when and if asked, could assist any of the church executives or any of the BEDC representatives anticipate the result of the actions which they were proposing to take.

In four instances, the crisis team furnished consultants with conflict resolution skills who were able to supply perceptions which obviously influenced decisions made by agencies in response to the demands and threats. These responses moderated the destructive aspect of the confrontations and recognized the opportunities the crisis offered to the agencies and their programs.

The crisis team, coordinated by Miss Peggy Billings and Mrs. Carolyn Wilhelm McIntyre of the Women's Division, maintained a twenty-four-hour clearing house which at some strategic points was used to explore options and broker resources. The low-profile operation did not attempt to interfere with any of the negotiations. However, it did communicate information which apparently was useful to several groups as they sought to resolve a difficult situation.

Of course, I kept closely in touch with executives of the Board of Missions (Board of Global Ministries) and with the Board of Christian Social Concerns (Board of Church and Society). I also kept in daily contact with Dr. Ralph David Abernathy, president of the Southern Christian Leadership Conference, who had asked me to keep him informed.

Consequently, when I reported to Dr. Abernathy that one of the points of polarization in the discussion was the seeming non-

Christian and pro-Marxist introduction to the Black Manifesto, Dr. Abernathy and Rev. Andrew Young sent a telegram which placed the discussion in a new context. The telegram, timed to arrive at the National Council of Churches just before the executive committee was to consider a task force recommendation concerning the Black Manifesto, said:

> The churches have long been guilty of a lack of stewardship in institutions. We have invested in profit-making corporations without concern that those profits came from exploitation of our brethren in southern Africa, Asia or Latin America. We have allowed God's treasure to be used to develop weapons of death and destruction. We have failed to invest in housing for the poor, jobs for the jobless, and given only a pittance of those instrumentalities which labor for peace and justice among men . . . Now God has sent a crude but determined prophet to pledge us to repentance, and we debate his language, his methods and ignore his message. There can be but one question to debate in regard to the so-called Black Manifesto: Is our Lord speaking to us through it? We Black Christians have too often ignored the church and felt its power to be too limited or irrelevant in the principalities and powers of this age. Has God raised up this one from his own children of Abraham? These are questions to be discussed by men of faith, not a court of law. And if we discover that we are now the money changers in the temple of our Lord, can we but confess our sins and determine the nature of our repentance? We pray for you in this hour of discernment.

Barrages of other messages favoring a law enforcement response to Mr. Forman's challenge were received by the executives of the National Council of Churches and by the denominational officials. Since the leadership of Dr. Martin Luther King, Jr., and the work of the Southern Christian Leadership Conference had been supported in the past by the very churches responding to the chaos caused by the Black Manifesto, SCLC representatives believed it was the strategic time to send the message. Faith questions had to be raised when the use of force was being considered within the headquarters building of so many of the Christian denominations of the country.

When the enforcement of the injunction hung in the balance in the discussions which were taking place within the National Council of Churches, Dr. Abernathy also communicated through me the message that if there was an attempt made to arrest Mr. Forman within the Interchurch Center, that he, Dr. Abernathy, would come immediately to New York City and stand with Mr. Forman and also be subjected to arrest. I communicated this immediately to the NCC Executive Committee which was in session at the time. From our vantage point, it was not possible to know altogether how significant the telegram and Dr. Abernathy's message were as factors in determining the final response of the NCC committee and of the denominational representatives. But it did give an opportunity for discussion to continue and ultimately for tension to ease.

Easing that tension was important, for the Interchurch Center had within it all of the previolence signs I had seen in other places. A Department of Justice representative told me that the situation was so bad at one point that evangelist Billy Graham, who had been scheduled to come to a breakfast meeting within the Interchurch Center, had been advised by the Secret Service to cancel his plans.

Discreet behind-the-scenes options needed to be considered in order for the hardened positions to be sufficiently moderated. Otherwise, the kinds of flexible decisions that needed to be made on the spot could not have been accomplished.

One night Mr. Forman informed me that a federal grand jury had been convened in Detroit, investigating claims that the presentation of the Black Manifesto demands was an act of criminal extortion against the churches. Several lay and clerical persons from the churches had been subpoenaed to appear. Mr. Forman angrily asked, "And what are the churches going to do about that?" I called NCC officials that night and suggested that this would take the Black Manifesto debate from the churches and subject it to possible repressive actions on the part of the government. NCC officials responded the next morning by saying they would assist in furnishing adequate legal defense for any persons indicted by the federal grand jury and that National Council of

Churches' lawyers had been alerted to stand by to render their services if they were required. I communicated this to Mr. Forman. I believe that this action signaled to Mr. Forman NCC concern for him and his colleagues even though they had engaged NCC officials in hard debate about the charges and the demands incorporated in the Black Manifesto. I believe that this initiative provided the basis for the agreement reached between the church agencies and Mr. Forman and the BEDC which resulted lifting the restraining order and in continuing the debate.

The eight-to-ten-week period of tight negotiations within a tense setting in the Interchurch Center had many positive results. *First*, the Black Manifesto prompted the churches to examine their stewardship. It enacted a kind of "freedom of information" act within the churches, and for the first time a serious social inventory was made of the churches' investments. *Second*, the manifesto gave impetus to the reordering of priorities within the churches. Negotiations revealed that control of denominational resources was almost totally in the hands of whites. The employment of minority persons in decision-making positions was enhanced by the manifesto confrontation. *Third*, the Black Manifesto, with all of its threat of force and accusations of racism, probably served as one of the most effective educational materials distributed recently within the churches.

The Black Economic Development Conference did not receive any significant funding as a result, but the confrontation directly caused substantial amounts of money to be allocated within each of the denominations to minority programs and to community organizations, and it helped build support within churches for this type of funding.

Fourth, the successful use of the negotiation process rather than a law enforcement response preserved the integrity of the churches and enabled them to witness during future confrontations. If there had been violence in the Interchurch Center as the result of a police enforcement of a restraining order, what could the churches have said at the time of Kent State, Jackson State, Attica, and Wounded Knee?

The Black Manifesto may have made it possible for laity and

clergy of various denominations to understand some of the complexities which are met by denominational executives as they attempt to implement the policy of the church in faithfulness to the gospel of Jesus Christ. As the church itself was confronted, not only in New York, but in many other cities across the nation, a much sharper awareness was developed as to the social responsibility of the church and some of the difficult problems in trying to implement it.

8

Kent State and Jackson State

On May 4, 1970, I attended a meeting in New York of the National Alliance for Safer Cities, an organization founded through the initiative of the American Jewish Committee. Called to the phone, I learned that CBS News had just reported four students killed and nine others wounded by the Ohio National Guard on the campus of Kent State University shortly after noon. Soldiers, or quasi-soldiers, had fired at students. Antiwar protests had peaked. There had to be rapid and severe repercussions.

Finally, I could concentrate no more at the meeting and went to my hotel room. Tuning in CBS, I waited for Walter Cronkite's report on the evening newscast. The earlier flash was correct. Names and pictures of the dead flickered briefly—typical American college students. Then unbelievably came a commercial advertising Kent cigarettes—"Kent's got it all together." What happened at Kent State that day violently expressed what had been brewing for several months.

Students became the new targets of repression, primarily because they formed the continuing core of resistance to the administration's Vietnam policy. College students and representatives of the federal administration had been battling for some time. Words and demonstrations had turned into combat weapons lowered against the students—and on a college campus. It was a new phase; there was no turning back.

When three days before the Kent State shooting, President Nixon had used the word *bums* to describe protesting students, contrasting them to the young men who were loyally serving their country in Vietnam, I shuddered, "My God, doesn't he know the power of presidential words?" One federal commission had already described the process by which even municipal administrators subtly give signals to the police through their press statements and informal comments. These signals often have more impact than written policy or formal orders.

The newspapers reported that on Sunday, May 3—the day before the shooting—Ohio Governor James Rhodes went to the Kent State campus and made a speech even more provocative than the president's press statement. Governor Rhodes was a candidate for the Republican nomination for the United States Senate in a primary election to be held within two days. Certain student war protesters, he declared, were "worse than the brown shirts and the Communist element and all of the night riders and the vigilantes. They are the worst type of people that we harbor in America." He went on to assert that "we're going to use every weapon of the law enforcement agencies of Ohio to drive them out of Kent." A political speech was soon translated by others into a military command, subtly and silently.

On television, a grieving man, Arthur Krause, father of Allison Krause, one of the four students killed in the Ohio National Guard fusillade, asked: "Have we come to such a state in this country that a young girl has to be shot because she disagrees with the actions of her government? She resented being called a bum because she disagreed with someone else's opinion. She thought the war in Cambodia was wrong. Is this dissent a crime?"

He was emotional, and his words were powerful, but the real question was who would answer. Already there were calls for investigations. I assumed the facts would be determined.

Kent State haunted me. Students who had been *studying* were suddenly *dying*. I clipped the articles about the shooting. I tried to get more information, but the only certainty was that our nation was plunged into another serious crisis. A friend of mine at the Department of Justice described the administration's reaction as one of near panic. The Kent State incident stirred furious reactions among students on a thousand campuses. The president's immediate statement after the shooting, "When dissent turns to violence it invites tragedy," seemed to posthumously indict and convict the students who had been killed. This fanned the flame of outrage across the country.

The student reaction to the Kent State shooting exceeded the protests voiced when the president made his Cambodian "incursion" speech on the evening of April 30, the remarks that had initiated the protest at Kent and on other campuses. The aftermath of Kent State was not unlike the 1968 student-worker protest in France which had brought that nation to a complete standstill. There were differences, but the student strike that hit the United States in 1970 was unprecedented. No one could predict the direction it would take.

No wonder there was real fear in the highest places of national government after May 4.

On May 6, 1970, two days after the killings, Secretary of the Interior Walter J. Hickel wrote to the president saying, "Today our young people, or at least a vast segment of them, believe they have no opportunity to communicate with government, regardless of administration, other than through violent confrontation. But I'm convinced we—and they—have the capacity, if we will but have the willingness to learn from history." Mr. Hickel's advice was not well received in the White House, and his "word of understanding" about the outcries of students only created misunderstanding between himself and the president. John Ehrlichman, the president's adviser for domestic affairs, called to tell Mr. Hickel that he would be unwelcome at the White House Sunday services thereafter.

The Washington *Post* reported that the White House had been barraged by messages in the days since the Kent shooting. "A few hours after the volley of gunfire at Kent State University, Robert Finch's telephone rang and the voice of his daughter Maureen cried out from across the continent at Occidental College in California. 'What are we going to do Daddy?' she asked, 'You don't know what is happening here.' "

John Ehrlichman's son called him from Stanford University. George Schultz's daughter called him from the University of Denver.

The article described these and other calls as the activation of "an extraordinary and extremely powerful private network of communications" and noted that "the upset of the last two weeks has been different. It has come home to those in government in very personal ways because of the intercession of real people."

The fact that the article is published in the May 15, 1970, edition is significant. It was being printed simultaneously with another shooting taking place on the campus of Jackson State College in Mississippi. Shortly after midnight, at approximately 12:10 A.M., two students were killed and twelve wounded. The knot in the pit of my stomach since the Kent State shooting tightened. The generations were at war.

News reports indicated that Alexander Hall, a girls' dormitory, had been raked with gunfire from the first to the fifth floors in a barrage laid down by the Mississippi Highway Patrol and the Jackson city police. Official reports later revealed that thirty-eight patrolmen of the Mississippi Highway Patrol and five officers of the Jackson police department had fired at the dormitory in a fusillade lasting twenty-eight seconds. They fired thirty-five shotguns, five military carbines, two machine guns, and one .308 rifle at a range of twenty yards. In that twenty-eight seconds, one hundred to one hundred fifty rounds were fired containing eight hundred to one thousand separate projectiles. Thirty shotguns fired double-O-buckshot, each shell containing nine pellets with a diameter of a .30 caliber bullet.

Immediately before the firing, Lt. Magee of the Jackson police had ordered the students to disperse. They started scattering across the lawn, running toward the dormitory entrance. Then, according to reports, a brick was thrown, a bottle smashed in the streets, and there was a cry of "sniper." The fusillade was then unleashed. Gunfire covered the front of the dormitory but concentrated on the stairwell. Every pane of glass was shattered. The metal panels between the floors were perforated by hundreds of bullets and pellets of buckshot.

Two black young men were killed: Phillip Gibbs, a twenty-year-old junior and father of an eighteen-month-old son, from Ripley, Mississippi, and James Earl Green, a Jackson, Mississippi, high-school student.

Phillip had just returned to the campus from visiting his wife and family the previous weekend. He had taken parental vows at the baptism of his son in St. Paul United Methodist Church on Mother's Day, May 10, 1970. Two pellets entered his brain. James Earl Green was on the opposite side of the street, in front of the Roberts Dining Hall, taking his usual route home from a job in a near-campus sandwich shop, when he was killed. The twelve wounded students were on the lawn, on the stairwell, and in the TV lounge of the dormitory.

Following the shooting, a cloud of fear covered the entire city of Jackson. The outrage erupting among the students and within the black community was unprecedented in the city's history, even though the capital of the state of Mississippi previously had experienced all kinds of racial violence. A businessman from Jackson called our office in Washington. He said to me, "We need you to come right down. I have lived in Jackson for more than twenty years, and I have seen this town experience nearly everything. This is the worst. Something has to be done, or this city is really going to blow."

I flew to Jackson the next day and began working with Robert Lamb, Jr. and other representatives of the Community Relations Service. For the next two weeks I worked in the lowest possible profile, and the assignment stretched around the clock.

Once more we set up a crisis center and initiated a systematic process of working all possible contacts and checking all available sources of information. To determine whether the church should take strategic steps, I worked closely with CRS representatives who moved carefully and skillfully on their own assignments.

It became unmistakably clear that the crisis in Jackson stemmed from the separate and opposing responses made by the mayor of Jackson. Russell Davis, and by the governor of the state of Mississippi, John Bell Williams. The mayor, a moderate, had been in office less than nine months, succeeding Allen B. Thompson, who had occupied the office for twenty-five years, described by many blacks as an arch-segregationist. Mayor Davis had expressed his sympathy to the families of the victims of the shooting and publicly characterized the day of the shooting as "the saddest day of my life." He was in communication with an ad hoc organization, the Concerned Citizens and Students of Jackson, which had emerged immediately in the black community. He was attempting to deal with their grievances. The governor made a different kind of public statement, provocative and threatening.

The immediate and most explosive issue was the state's proposed removal of the bullet-punctured metal panels from the front of Alexander Hall. Pictures showing the five stories of the dormitory, with smashed windows, perforated panels, and pocked masonry, went over the wire to all parts of the country and appeared on front pages of newspapers everywhere. They had been an embarrassment to the governor who was determined to replace the panels promptly. Students adamantly refused to let them be taken down, convinced that the state would destroy the evidence. The evidence had to be preserved, and it would become a memorial to the two dead young men.

They were on a collision course. The state had the power, but the students stood fast. The students maintained a twenty-four-hour vigil in front of the dormitory. Even though all classes at Jackson State had been suspended for the remainder of the spring quarter a few hours after the shooting, many students remained. With black armbands, they took their angry stance. Signs erected in front of Alexander Hall declared, "No physical evidence to be removed!" Another sign was printed, "One picture is worth a thousand words." Others simply said, "Jackson State College is not Vietnam" and "Campus Slaughterhouse for Students."

The situation was dangerous. The governor declared that the state would take the panels. The mayor attempted to negotiate, but he was uncertain of his final authority under these circumstances and of the strength of his political support. In the long shadow cast from the state house, negotiations with students continued. The Federal Bureau of Investigaton might take possession of the panels instead of the state of Mississippi. Although this proposal was finally acceptable to the students, they insisted that nothing be dismantled, repaired, or replaced until after the funeral of James Earl Green, scheduled for Friday, May 22. The funeral of Phillip Gibbs had been conducted in private earlier in Ripley.

As the contest continued, it was plain that the mayor needed support. I talked with the layman who had summoned me to Jackson about the possibility of an emergency meeting with the businessmen of the city where the critical factors could be raised. At a hastily called meeting, CRS representatives briefed the business community fully on every aspect of the crisis. A nearly unanimous vote of support for the mayor was tabulated, then communicated privately and discreetly to the governor. In a climate of violence, the scale started to tip toward moderation. Yet the state continued to hurl threats at students standing vigil in front of Alexander Hall on the state-owned campus. The governor had one thousand National Guard troops on ready alert. He might move even against the advice of the powerful business community of the capital.

The situation was a powder keg. Jackson State College students were determined that the dormitory panels remain in place until the funeral of James Earl Green. Congressmen and other dignitaries attending the funeral could see for themselves what had taken place on May 15. The students were in a precarious position. At this point we suggested to some faculty members of Millsaps College, a predominantly white United Methodist college in Jackson, that it would be strategic for white students to communicate direct support for the students at Jackson State. A floral piece, with a card of sympathy, arrived in front of Alexander Hall within an hour. More importantly, however, a number of Millsaps students began to stand in rotation with the Jackson State students. This balancing mechanism was very much needed. Many Millsaps students had expressed concern but did not know that they were wanted or urgently needed on the Jackson State campus. The passed word broadened the protest base, and as it did, tension lessened.

James Earl Green's burial was scheduled for one week after he was killed. The days and nights between May 15 and May 22 were long and filled with grief and anxiety. Rumors shot back and forth between the white and black communities. The Rumor Control Center set up by Mrs. Marge Curet of the Community Relations Service, in cooperation with a labor union, operated around the clock to counter false reports. CRS representatives moved throughout the city to have accurate information as worried citizens telephoned the center. Sometimes the callers repeated rumors which, if true, represented dangerous developments. Stories were checked out quickly and quietly until the facts were nailed down. On the night before the funeral, the governor delivered a television address in which he warned of the possibility of violence and stated the measures he proposed to quell it. The mayor delivered his own hasty address a short time later to counter the ominous words from the governor's mansion. Mayor Davies had won the point that security for the city of Jackson on the day of the funeral would be in his hands. The governor assumed the mayor was making a mistake. He was just waiting for the reaction; then he would move.

James Earl Green's funeral was at 2:00 P.M. on May 22, at the M. W. Stringer Masonic Temple, 1072 Lynch Street, a short distance from Jackson State's campus. Memorial services for Emmett Till and Medgar Evers had been held in the same hall.

The Jackson city police were regularly patroling the area shortly after noon. Their presence was heavy but kept at a careful distance. Weapons were prominently displayed in scout car windows, but I interpreted this as a necessary signal to the state as much as a warning to people attending the funeral who might be planning violent action.

The white hearse from the Collins Funeral Home brought James Earl Green's body to the Masonic Temple shortly after 1:00 P.M. Attendants wheeled the casket into the front of the hall, and after they opened it, a long line of mourners began filing past. I walked in that line, and as I moved down the aisle, I remembered walking in a similar line to view the body of Dr. Martin Luther King, Jr. It all felt the same although two years had passed, and now a boy's body lay in the casket. The obituary in the memorial folder handed me by a white-gloved usher as I entered the hall simply said, "James Earl Green was born December 19, 1952 in Jackson, Mississippi, to the union of Mrs. Mertle Green Burton and the late Mr. Willie Green. He was the fifth of nine children. He received his education at Esable Elementary School. He continued his education at Jim Hill High School where he was a member of the track team. He was to be graduated in June, 1970."

As I sat in the balcony, I watched the hall fill up. People took every seat and stood in the aisles along the walls. In the stifling hot temple the congregation waited quietly. Two o'clock arrived, but the funeral did not begin because congressmen who had flown down from Washington for the funeral were stopping at Alexander Hall to see for themselves the bullet-riddled girls' dormitory. The student vigil had worked, and the pellet-perforated panels were still in place.

After the congressmen arrived on the platform, the Mt. Nebo Missionary Baptist Church choir filed in, and the family of James Earl Green was escorted to their seats. The service began.

Deep and dignified grief flooded the Masonic Temple that day. When the service ended and the casket was placed in the hearse by the pallbearers, the crowd filed out and proceeded on foot to the cemetery. The hearse moved slowly, and three thousand people marched behind it. Police, positioned at close intervals, blocked off the route. Patrol cars also circled the side streets.

We moved down Lynch Street, past Alexander Hall and the Roberts Dining Hall, through the campus of Jackson State College. The sun was bright, the afternoon hot. Most of us took off our coats and carried them. Block by block we walked until we reached the cemetery across the street from Jim Hill High School. The service at the grave was brief, and soon the dreaded day—the day of expected violence—was ended. There was no violence. Those who mourned the death of James Earl Green, a high-school student who had been gunned down on his way home from a part-time job, had walked through a corridor of guns to pay their respects. Still there was no violence.

Many colleges cut short their spring terms after the Kent State and Jackson State shootings, and most college administrators looked toward the fall with ever-deepening anxiety. On June 13,

President Nixon named a nine-member Commission on Campus Unrest, chaired by the former governor of Pennsylvania, William W. Scranton. The commission first met on June 25 and was instructed to complete its work within three months, submitting a report before the beginning of the fall semester. After the president's Commission on Campus Unrest finished its hearings in Jackson, it concluded that "the 28 second fusillade from police officers was an *unreasonable, unjustified overreaction*" (italics added).

The Scranton commission made note of the conflicting evidence about the existence of a sniper. The FBI reported, after examining the third-floor stairwell window from which the sniper fire was supposed to have originated, "that all observable bullet holes in the window were made by shots from outside the building."

Furthermore, the commission stated that "racial animosity on the part of white police officers was a substantial contributing factor" in the deaths and injuries of the students.[1]

A federal grand jury completed its investigation of the Jackson State shooting four and one-half months later, but no indictments were brought against any law enforcement officer. A spokesman for the Justice Department said, "In view of the irreconcilably conflicting evidence bearing on whether the officers could reasonably believe they were being fired upon by a sniper, it was not believed by Civil Rights Division attorneys, the United States Attorney, or by the grand jury, that the government could prove beyond a reasonable doubt that these officers fired into the dormitory with the *specific intent* to deprive persons there of their rights."

The criminal law route was closed. Constance Slaughter, staff attorney for the Lawyers' Committee for Civil Rights Under Law, filed a $13.8 million civil suit against state and city officials and law enforcement officers. On March 22, 1972, the trial jury gave a verdict in favor of the defendants. An appeal was filed with the United States Court of Appeals for the Fifth Circuit. The appeals

1. The President's Commission on Campus Unrest, p. 450.

court upheld the jury's verdict on the grounds that it could not be shown that any specific officer was "an actual cause of harm to any plaintiff." Nevertheless, the court stated that "the barrage of gunfire far exceeded the response that was appropriate for a detachment the size of this one and for under the circumstances it faced. This conclusion is not judicial second guessing of officers faced with danger, rendered from the quiet and safety of judges' chambers. It is what the evidence shows."

An appeal to the United States Supreme Court was not heard.

9

Not Another Kent State!

In May, 1970, Ohio National Guardsmen fired their rifles at Kent State students protesting U.S. involvement in Cambodia. Today, looking down from the hill where the guardsmen stood, you can see a stone marker standing at the edge of the Prentice Hall parking lot. It lists, "In Living Memory," the names of the four students who died that day: Allison Krause, Jeffrey Miller, Sandra Scheuer, and William Schroeder.

Other words have also been etched into the American mind: "Not Another Kent State!" These words describe disapproval of the automatic use of gunfire to control unpopular expressions of dissent. They are now a part of the American subconscious, and they have affected the policy decisions of many law enforcement officials as they prepared for demonstrations and confrontations of protest.

The memory of Kent State and the insistence that there be no repetition of what happened there remain largely because of the extraordinary efforts of two tenacious men: Arthur Krause and Peter Davies.

The death certificate of Allison Krause, nineteen-year-old daughter of Arthur and Doris, lists the cause of death as "gunshot wound with massive hemorrhage and penetration of the left lower lobe of lung, spleen, stomach, duodenum, liver and inferior vena cava. Wounds caused by bullets similar to .30 caliber military ammunition." Her body had been ripped apart by a bullet fired from an M-1 combat rifle supplied to the Ohio National Guard by the United States Government. Her father wanted to know why.

Peter Davies, however, knew none of the students who were killed at Kent State. In fact, he had never even heard of the university before the incident. A New York insurance broker who came to the United States from England in 1957, Davies was horrified by the shooting and wrote a letter of protest to President Nixon which began, "To die for dissent in a democracy is the ultimate tragedy." Along with a copy of the letter, Davies sent a note of sympathy to Mr. and Mrs. Krause. When Allison's father called Davies to express the family's appreciation, the two men joined in a difficult and painful crusade for justice.

Competing investigations were conducted by the president's Commission on Campus Unrest, the Federal Bureau of Investigation, the inspector general's office of the Ohio National Guard, the Ohio State Highway Patrol, the Special Kent State University Commission on KSU Violence, the American Civil Liberties Union, and various other groups.

Their conclusions conflicted. On September 26, the president's Commission on Campus Unrest reported that "the indiscriminate firing of rifles into a crowd of students and the deaths that followed [at Kent State] were unnecessary, unwarranted and inexcusable." Yet, on October 16, the Ohio Special Grand Jury declared the National Guard blameless in the deaths and injuries of the Kent State students, held the university administration responsible for the disturbance, and proceeded to indict twenty-five students and faculty.

Later in October a complete summary of the eight-thousand-page FBI investigative report, written by staff attorneys of the Criminal Section of the Civil Rights Division of the U.S. Department of Justice, was made public. According to the summary: The assembly of students which the guard attempted to disperse was peaceful and quiet until the guard advanced. The guard had not been surrounded. There was no sniper. There was reason to believe that the claim by the guard that their lives were endangered by the students was fabricated subsequent to the event.

The discrepancies between the conclusions reached by the Ohio Special Grand Jury and the evidence gathered by three hundred FBI agents caused Arthur Krause to turn toward the United States Department of Justice and members of Congress for answers. Yet, weeks went by, the months began to mount, and the federal government did not reply to his appeal for action. By the latter part of February, 1971, Krause began to fear that the Kent State case would soon be closed.

The Washington *Post* on Sunday, March 21, 1971, included an article by Ken W. Clawson, later deputy director of communications in the Nixon White House, announcing that

> The government has virtually decided against convening a federal grand jury to investigate the killing of four Kent State University students by Ohio National Guardsmen last May. Only final approval by Attorney General John N. Mitchell is needed to ratify a decision, reached reluctantly by the Justice Department's Civil Rights Division that the government should not enter the case.

Coincidentally, the day before the article appeared, I had been on the Kent State campus. A minister from Akron, where I had been on an assignment, took me to the campus to speak with some students, professors, and clergy about their firsthand reactions to the shooting and their concern about the conclusions reached in the investigations conducted by the state of Ohio. After the discussion, I wandered into the university book store to browse over recent publications and was immediately struck by a title which underlined the meeting I had just attended: *Confrontation at Kent State—13 Seconds*, written by two Cleveland *Plain Dealer* reporters, Joe Eszterhas and Michael Roberts.

I purchased the book to read on the trip back to Washington, and as I concentrated on it, my idea of events at Kent State clarified, and I began to develop pictures of the persons whose lives were twisted or ended in those dreadful days. When I picked up the Washington *Post* the next morning and read Clawson's article, saying that the federal government probably would not act on the case, I reacted with an audible, "No! No, we cannot accept that decision."

Monday morning I telephoned Cleveland author Michael Roberts, asked whether he had seen Clawson's article, and arranged to meet him to discuss any steps the church might take. He suggested that I call one of the parents—Arthur Krause. I hesitated. "Mike," I said, "I don't want to add to his trouble. The parents have had enough already."

"Go ahead and call him," Mike replied. "He will want to talk with you. I can assure you of that." He gave me Krause's office and home telephone numbers; I waited to call him at his home in Pittsburgh that evening.

The telephone conversation was described by Arthur Krause in an interview with Wesley Pruden, Jr., of the *National Observer* (August 18, 1973):

> I was pretty low when I heard the news from Washington (in 1971) that the Justice Department had decided not to prosecute anyone. . . . Then Peter Davies called from New York to suggest that maybe the churches would help. Basically what I was getting from the churches was sympathy. I was so tired of that word. Sympathy was not what we wanted. "Peter," I told him, "I don't think there is a God." Just then my daughter handed me a note saying "A Reverend John Adams in Washington is trying to get in touch with you." I called him back and he invited me down to Washington.

Fifteen hours later Mr. and Mrs. Arthur Krause were in my office in Washington, D.C., to meet with the Task Force on Civil Liberties of the Washington Interreligious Staff Committee, a coalition of Washington-based legislative representatives of various religious denominations. We decided that a small group of denominational representatives would consult with constitutional lawyers and former Justice Department attorneys and then approach the Civil Rights Division. Contacts were made immediately, and within forty-eight hours we met with Assistant Attorney General Jerris Leonard, head of the Civil Rights Division of the Department of Justice.

Leonard told us that no decision had been made concerning closing the Kent State case but conceded that the Washington

Post article was otherwise correct in its statement that the case might be closed. We appealed to him to use a federal grand jury to complete the Kent State investigation on the grounds that each of the other investigations had been stopped from obtaining available evidence or even necessary information. He told us our suggestions would be officially considered.

We waited a month, but there was no indication that the Justice Department was proceeding with a review of the case. The Kent State matter was no longer mentioned in the newspapers. When we telephoned the Civil Rights Division, we received only vague responses to our pointed questions.

Our small committee needed considerably more information to make a stronger and more concrete proposal to the Justice Department. I tried to gather information quickly by telephoning government officials, newspaper reporters, and Arthur Krause. Arthur referred me to Peter Davies who had developed an encyclopedic knowledge of the Kent State event.

Davies had poured over the official and unofficial investigative reports of the shooting and had tracked down every bit of available information. He had also collected some shreds of evidence which did not appear in any of the reports. He had spent hours analyzing and comparing the thousands of photographs which had been taken on May 4. Peter had become so knowledgeable that he was being used as a reference service by the attorneys retained by the families of the students for the civil suits filed against the state of Ohio and individual public officials. At once, Peter sent a flow of information to my office.

I also contacted the parents and families of the other Kent State victims, discovering that they didn't know one another and had not consulted one another about the incident. The grief they were still experiencing was compounded by the expression of public support given to the National Guard action in which their children had been killed and wounded. Newspaper interviews and letters revealed that an extraordinary large number of people felt that the students "had it coming to them."

I brought the families together. At first, there was only hurt and hesitancy. However, as parents and surviving students shared information and sorrow, they began to build a common commitment. They believed that a federal grand jury should be convened for the purpose of investigating the shootings.

Our office became a coordinating center for the families and their attorneys. Carol Ross, our program assistant, activated a telephone network which maintained the flow of information to every family. We realized that it could all end precisely at the point at which the Jackson State case had ended before a federal grand jury. However, unlike the Jackson State shooting of which there was no photograhic record, there were more than three thousand photographs of Kent State as well as some motion pictures taken by students, faculty members, and newspaper photographers, giving an accurate step-by-step account of the movement of the students and the actions of the National Guard.

Davies worked long hours every day sorting and sifting the facts which he extracted from the investigative materials. Arthur Krause maintained a steady stream of telephone calls to White House aides, members of Congress and their staff assistants, Justice Department attorneys, and news reporters. The families began to enlist some political support in Washington, D.C., for a continuing investigation. While there was no announcement from the Department of Justice, unconfirmed reports concerning the Justice Department's intention to close the Kent State case continued. In the middle of May, 1971, I decided to telephone Deputy Attorney General Richard Kleindeinst whom I had consulted on two previous issues. He was unavailable, but I left a message, and late that same afternoon after our office had closed and I continued to work, the phone rang. I picked it up, and a voice said, "Hello, John. This is Dick."

"Dick?" I hesitantly responded.

"Dick—Dick Kleindeinst," the caller replied. I hadn't remembered Mr. Kleindeinst speaking with me on a first-name basis in previous contacts, and I was slightly taken aback. Perhaps, I thought, he was resorting to the "first-name tactic" some had described, which is used by high-level officials to overpower persons who make inquiries on delicate issues.

I gulped once and then continued, "Mr. Kleindeinst, I am calling about the Kent State case. The families keep hearing that the Justice Department is going to close it, and yet they are now convinced after having checked the available reports, that there are questions which simply have not been answered. If the federal government doesn't deal with them, they are convinced that no one else will." He expressed words of sympathy for their families, said that he believed he understood their feelings, and then described the restrictions under which the federal government was working.

I persisted, "If it is impossible for the Justice Department to do anything further on the Kent State case, should not this be interpreted to the families? Wouldn't it be better for them to have an interpretation from the government rather than reading an announcement of the closing of the case in the newspapers? Could representatives of the families come to Washington and have Justice Department attorneys explain to them the problems which prevent any further action?"

"I don't think that such a meeting would be useful to the families or the department," he said. "It would be too emotionally charged. However, I would meet with you and with one of the attorneys for the families. Let them select one attorney, and then you call my office, and we will arrange a meeting."

Two days later attorney Steven Sindell, who represented several of the families, and I met with Kleindeinst for more than an hour. The outcome of the discussion was another appointment to be scheduled with the new assistant attorney general for the Civil Rights Division, David Norman. Kleindeinst asked us to prepare a report for Norman enumerating the points we wanted to cover. Peter Davies set aside his insurance business for a month and worked day and night to complete the 227-page report which included more than seventy significant photographs. The Board of Church and Society printed ninety copies. On June 21, 1971, the report was given to Norman who said he would need time for his staff to evaluate the materials before he could respond further. Copies were then delivered to the offices of Attorney General John N. Mitchell, Deputy General Richard Kleindeinst, William Scranton, members of the president's Commission on Campus

Unrest, attorney general for the state of Ohio, the Portage County prosecutor, and to a large number of church representatives.

Davies' report, entitled "An Appeal to the United States Department of Justice for an Immediate and Thorough Investigation of the Circumstances Surrounding the Shootings at Kent State University," suggested that on the basis of the evidence so far available, that it was possible that some Ohio National Guardsmen had conspired to shoot at the students and that specific guardsmen had triggered and participated in the shooting. The appeal asked for a federal grand jury to investigate the matter.

A month passed, but there was still no indication of a review by the Civil Rights Division. I received word that Attorney General Mitchell had definitely decided to close the case and was waiting for Congress to recess for the summer in order to make public his decision. We decided to release the appeal to the public. On the evening of July 22, excerpts of the report were read by Walter Cronkite on CBS Evening News. The next day newspapers across the country carried portions of the new Kent State report.

Reactions poured into our office in Washington. "What concern should it be to the United Methodist church whether or not there was a conspiracy? What possible religious significance is there?" The reactions about the church's involvement were overwhelmingly negative. Our reply firmly stated our conviction: When loaded rifles are used in a civil disorder in violation of the Department of Army guidelines for the use of such force, the church, as well as other parts of society, must insist that there be accountability. When there is a summary execution of persons protesting governmental policy, the basic constitutional rights of every citizen are in jeopardy.

We saw, not just denominational interest in the issue, but deep religious significance: human life had been violated by the government.

Many felt it would have been easier for our agency to justify its involvement if one of the young people who had been killed was a United Methodist. But when it was determined that none of those fatally injured on May 4, 1970, was a member of the United Methodist church, additional questions were raised about the agency's involvement.

Shortly after the appeal for justice was released, a *Time* magazine reporter telephoned the Krause home and Laurie, Allison's younger sister, answered the call. Arthur and Doris Krause were out for the evening. "Well, perhaps you can answer a question for me," the *Time* representative said. "Just how high up in the United Methodist church is your father?"

Laurie paused a moment, trying to understand the question, and then answered, "We're Jewish."

The issue was larger than any church or any one religion. It was not a matter of being antilaw enforcement or negative toward the National Guard; it was rather the fact of maintaining lawful responses to the exercise of the constitutional right "to petition the government for a redress of grievances."

On Friday, August 13, 1971, one day after Congress had recessed for summer vacation, Attorney General John Mitchell held a press conference and stated:

> The facts available to me support the conclusion reached by the President's Commission that the rifle fire was, in the words of the Commission, "unnecessary, unwarranted, and inexcusable." However, our review persuades me that there is no credible evidence of a conspiracy between National Guardsmen to shoot students on the campus and that there is no likelihood of successful prosecution of individual guardsmen.
>
> . . . it appears clear that further investigation by a federal grand jury could not reasonably be expected to produce any new evidence which would contribute further to making a prosecutive judgment . . .

For over a year the families of the victims, a number of Kent State students, and a few representatives of the churches continued their appeal, petitioning the White House, congressional committees, and the Department of Justice. Almost everyone else assumed that the case was finally closed. The Ohio National Guard particularly concluded the case was terminated, for in September, 1971, a noncommissioned officer filed a $1.5 million libel and slander suit against Peter Davies. Nine days later the complaint was amended adding the Board of Church and Society of the United Methodist Church as a defendant and asking for $3 million in damages.

Three and one half years later, on March 31, 1975, federal judge Constance Baker Motley, in the Southern District of New York, ordered the libel suit against Mr. Davies and the Board of Church and Society of the United Methodist Church which had been filed on September 13, 1971, dismissed. She stated: "If ever there was a case that deserved to be dismissed for lack of prosecution, this is it."

The libel suit did not alter the board's involvement in the Kent State issue in any respect. We continued to support Davies' work and kept in close touch with each family as we searched for ways to change government policy. Dean Kahler, the most seriously injured of those who survived the Kent State shooting, and a corps of Kent State students led by Paul Keane and Greg Rambo joined our crusade, soliciting signatures and petitions urging the Department of Justice to convene a grand jury. Actually, the libel suit probably helped us, for it showed the students that an institution which was definitely a part of the establishment shared in their freshly experienced vulnerability. After Kent State and Jackson State, a large part of the entire student generation began to feel exposed and defenseless. All students died a little that spring.

T-shirts with large bull's-eyes and the words "Kent State University" printed on them were worn on campuses around the country. Even high-school students felt vulnerable. One wrote to Peter Davies: "I live in a very conservative house. I didn't dare wear an armband of mourning when the students were killed, the best I could manage was wearing a red ribbon in my hair for a month, red for blood. I cried, but most of all I was afraid because if they could kill Allison and Jeffrey and Sandra and Bill, 'get away with it,' and have no one even care, what would stop them from hurting me . . ."

There was a sense of betrayal and hopelessness, a feeling that to speak up would mean being shot up, and the only way to prevent being shot up was to shut up.

Yet, months before the Kent State shooting President Nixon had declared in a speech at General Beadle State College, in

Madison, South Dakota, "The process of freedom will be less threatened in America . . . if we pay more heed to one of the great cries of the young today. I speak now of their demand for honesty: intellectual honesty, personal honesty, public honesty. Most of what seems to be revolt is little more than this: an attempt to strip away sham and pretense, to puncture illusion, to get down to the basic nub of truth. We should welcome this."[1]

In 1969, youth were calling for honesty, but by the fall of 1970, young people were running for cover. Ironically, as we worked on the Kent State case, we discovered that many young people not only lacked trust in "the system," they did not even trust those who believed the system could be made to work. Some students considered our appeal for a federal grand jury dangerous, leading to one more "put-down" of students, if not by guns, then by other destructive actions.

Some students were certain that *we*, rather than they, would learn something about "the system." The student who was with Allison at Kent State on the day she was shot to death wrote to Arthur Krause:

> Don't you get run-a-rounds in your inquiries? Don't you sometimes feel like dropping the entire thing? You have more patience than I and will probably continue hacking away to unveil the truth longer than I ever could. But with time you will be exposed to more lies, more red tape, more injustice. For this reason only, I hope this thing takes a God-awfully long time. Not to kill your efforts, but to help you understand why kids today are beginning to live differently, why they are refusing to cooperate with people (governments) that lie, cheat, kill, distort truths to their own ends, and why some are resorting to violence . . . No, I don't agree with what they're doing, but I fully *understand* why.

Perhaps the most abominable and even immoral response to the killing of the students, and the one to which the parents were frequently subjected, was that the deaths ultimately quieted the campuses and restored some order in society. In the fall of 1970, when it was feared the campuses would be in turmoil, there was

1. New York *Times*, June 4, 1969.

calm. According to the Justice Department, the wave of protest was subsiding "because our young people feel they are being heard."

Whenever I heard persons justify the killing of students because it had the practical effect of ending mass protests on the campuses, I always thought of the April, 1971, issue of the *Reader's Digest*, which included a condensation of James Michener's book, *Kent State: What Happened and Why*. Right in the middle of the condensation was an Ortho Chevron Chemical Company advertisement for insecticides. The bold black letters declared, "The balance of nature is predicated on the fact that one thing dies so that another may live." The advertisement described with deadly accuracy the rationalization being used across the country to justify the killing of the students. The advertisement continued: "The proposition that concerns both of us is the unceasing struggle between desirable plant life and destructive insects . . . These are just a few of your enemies. There are literally thousands more. But don't lose hope. With broad spectrum defense like——insecticide, you can repeal about any invasion." If one changes the words a bit they would read "the unceasing struggle between desirable students and destructive radicals." If *insecticide* is changed to *gunfire*, many would agree that invasions had been repelled at Kent State and at Jackson State.

Mrs. Florence Schroeder, mother of Bill Schroeder who was fatally injured when shot in the back, 382 feet from the nearest guardsmen, explained the justification which was commonly given for the killing: "I think that for a lot of people in America, when the kids were shot at Kent, it was the same as getting revenge . . . They were shooting the Weathermen, they were shooting members of SDS; our four were symbolic, or the thirteen, let's put it that way, were symbolic of all the destruction that had come about. They think now that because of those shootings it has stopped everything and that justifies the killing in their mind. 'Well, we've killed four, but look at all that we've saved since then.' "

The campuses were quiet in the fall of 1970, but it was a silence of death rather than the calm of social stability. It was the stillness of terror rather than the peace of those who had confidence in persons of power. Students remained motionless because they believed that otherwise they would be moving targets. It was repose caused by repression.

Before the fearful eyes of anxious youth, the Kent State parents waged their campaign for justice, and their efforts helped change students' deep despair and broken trust into a hesitant hope and a tentative faith.

I heard the author, Elie Wiesel, survivor of the Nazi death camps, speak in Highland Park, Illinois, in the spring of 1975. Concerning despair he said, "Those who despair have given up on their people, and they can destroy the world."

The Kent State parents did not give up on our society or its system of government. They helped reconstruct its spirit by converting their grief into a search for justice. I often heard them say, "This government is the best on the face of the earth. We must help it function. We must make it work. We will keep 'Kent State' alive until it does."

My responsibility was to coordinate their plans from time to time, convening the families for semiannual strategy sessions, usually held in a hotel suite in Cleveland. Our meetings were closed and unpublicized. Once, however, when we arrived, we found the hotel marquee announcing in extremely large letters, "Welcome Rev. John P. Adams and the Kent State Families." After expressing appreciation to the management for their consideration, we requested that no billing be given in the future. The meetings were private; those who attended—attorneys, Kent State students and faculty members, clergymen and others—were only invited by the families when they wanted particular kinds of assistance for their political action.

Although Attorney General Mitchell had closed the Kent State case in 1971, the families planned a demonstration in Washington for the second anniversary of the shooting. They intended to hold vigils at both the White House and the Department of Justice Building. They were to stand with huge black wreaths and placards during the morning of May 4 and then present petitions at 12:24 P.M., the time of the 1970 shooting. A permit was obtained for the demonstration, and everything was set. However, on May 2, 1972, J. Edgar Hoover, director of the Federal Bureau of Investigation died, and his funeral was set for the noon hour on May 4.

We quickly telephoned the parents and after a short discussion decided that a protest demonstration on the day of Mr. Hoover's funeral would be indecorous. Plans were immediately cancelled. The wreaths were discarded, and the signs were finally thrown away, but parents and the students who had been scheduled to come from Kent State to support them were disappointed.

It had taken an extraordinary personal adjustment for the parents of the children killed at Kent State to agree to take part in a demonstration in Washington, D.C. It was a difficult thing for them to do. When their painfully conceived plans had to be cancelled because of Mr. Hoover's funeral, they sensed a peculiar irony. Nevertheless, they reasoned, if it had not been for the FBI investigation of the shooting and the summary of the investigative report which was written by the Criminal Section of the Civil Rights Division of the Department of Justice, they could not have proceeded as far as they had in determining the truth about Kent State.

The day after Mr. Hoover's funeral, I received a telephone call from a high official of the FBI. He said, "Mr. Adams, I would like you to convey to the parents the appreciation which we have at the bureau for the cancellation of the demonstration. We want them to know that we recognized the gesture of respect toward the director."

A few days later, however, the families and their student supporters were back at the business of confronting government and voicing their appeal for a renewed investigation.

There was nothing accidental about the reappearance of the Kent State issue. A network of people, led by the families of the victims, concentrated on keeping the issue before the public until the government finally responded.

Ultimately the efforts of the families made an impact upon the American public. A Harris survey reported that "by 55 to 31 percent, Americans now agree that the National Guard shooting at rioting students at Kent State University which resulted in 4 deaths was 'unjustified and repressive.' In 1970, by a narrow 40–39 percent margin, the public had condoned the Kent State shootings as 'necessary and justified.' "[2]

Peter Davies continued to cull every piece of information, every scrap of evidence, and there was a volume of it being channeled to him from cooperative reporters and strategically located and interested citizens. In 1972, he began to reorganize the material of the appeal for justice into a manuscript for a book. Six different publishers showed serious interest until they learned of the libel complaint which had been filed against Davies and the church. Davies wrote to *Publisher's Weekly*, challenging the publishing companies to print a book which would call the government to account in the Kent State case. He received a reply from Henry Robbins of Farrar, Straus, and Giroux, and within weeks a contract was signed with Peter Davies *and* the Board of Church and Society of the United Methodist Church as co-authors. *The Truth about Kent State* was published in September, 1973.

In the wake of Watergate, Attorney General Richard Kleindeinst resigned from office. When Elliott Richardson was appointed attorney general, a new ray of hope began to strike those who had sought a federal grand jury. Three years and three months after the shooting, two years after the case had been closed, August 3, 1973, Richardson authorized the reopening of the investigation, and Assistant Attorney General J. Stanley Pottinger began to review the case. When the families met in Cleveland on September 16, 1973, I hand-delivered a letter from Mr. Pottinger to the parents which asked for their cooperation in furnishing every possible bit of additional information for the Justice Department's consideration.

When the "Saturday Night Massacre," as it was called, took place on October 20, 1973, and Attorney General Richardson resigned rather than follow President Nixon's order to fire Special Prosecutor Archibald Cox, the families again became concerned about the future of the investigation. William B. Saxbe, a former officer in the Ohio National Guard, was nominated as the new

2. Washington *Post*, September 27, 1973.

attorney general; so the families took a direct interest in Saxbe's confirmation hearings before the Senate Judiciary Committee. Again, it was far from coincidental that the first question posed to Mr. Saxbe in the hearings inquired about a public statement he had made suggesting termination of the new investigation. Saxbe promptly stated that he would disqualify himself entirely from the Kent State case. Before Saxbe was confirmed by the United States Senate, Acting Attorney General Robert Bork authorized the convening of a federal grand jury in the Northern District of Ohio to investigate the Kent State shooting.

The grand jury sat for 39 days, heard 173 witnesses, looked at 250 exhibits, and produced a transcript of 6,800 pages. On March 29, 1974, eight indictments were handed down against one present and seven former members of the Ohio National Guard. They were charged with "aiding and abetting each other" when they "did willfully assault and intimidate persons who were inhabitants of the State of Ohio . . . by willfully discharging loaded .30 caliber, M-1 rifles, at, over, into and in the direction of said persons, and did thereby willfully deprive said persons of the right secured and protected by the Constitution and laws of the United States not to be deprived of liberty without due process of law; and death resulted to the said Allison Krause, Jeffrey Miller, Sandra Scheuer, and William Schroeder from such deprivation."

After the Department of Justice presented the case for the prosecution in a trial in the fall of 1974, federal judge Frank J. Battisti, on November 8, 1974, granted a motion for acquittal of all eight guardsmen, stating that the government had not proven beyond a reasonable doubt that the eight defendants possessed the *specific intention* to deprive students of their Constitutional rights as required under Section 18 United States Code, Paragraph 242. That did not mean that the guardsmen had not fired their weapons, and it certainly did not imply that they had not targeted individual students. As a matter of fact, the judge stated in his opinion, "Some of the guardsmen fired at *specific students* while others merely fired into or over the crowd" (italics added).

Law, as interpreted by Judge Battisti, requires that the government prove *willful intent* to deprive a person of his civil rights when a law enforcement officer or, as in this case, a National Guardsman kills a person "under color of law." In other words, it is possible to shoot to kill without shooting to deprive an individual of his civil rights. Presumably, a person can be dead after such a shooting and still have his civil rights intact.

The state of Ohio, with energetic prosecution, could have pursued the case under its own criminal code, but this would have required the state to prosecute its own officials, and this was not done. There had been no route to take but the limited law related to federal civil rights.

Judge Battisti warned, therefore, "It is vital that state and National Guard officials not regard this decision as authorizing or approving the use of force against unarmed demonstrators, whatever the occasion of the issues. *Such use of force is, and was, deplorable*" (italics added).

The official words echo from both Jackson State and Kent State: "Unreasonable, unjustified overreaction"—"unnecessary, unwarranted, and inexcusable"—"deplorable." The point is that there is little protection for a citizen when he is confronted by an irresponsible law enforcement official operating "under color of law."

The criminal law, as interpreted, was narrow and not exercised within the states; so the families had recourse only within the civil court. On April 17, 1974, the United States Supreme Court reversed two lower courts that had held that state officials in Ohio were immune from civil suits for damages in the deaths and injuries of the students at Kent State. Chief Justice Warren E. Burger wrote the opinion for the justices who voted without dissent that the families of the dead and wounded had the right to a trial on the merits of the charges that the civil rights of the students had been violated.

In the spring of 1975, as the civil trial was approaching, an appeal for contributions to a Kent State Due Process of Law Fund was made by the Board of Church and Society of the United Methodist Church. The state of Ohio had already disbursed more than six hundred thousand dollars in the defense of the guardsmen and the state officials who were involved in the Kent State action. The families of the victims had no source of funds other than the contributions of individuals, small grants from church agencies, and approximately ten thousand dollars from the Playboy Foundation. However, legal bills, excluding any fees to lawyers, had accumulated and totaled more than one hundred thousand dollars.

Within four months more than two hundred fifty thousand dollars had been received from more than twenty thousand contributors. Many sent warm letters of concern, promising additional support. However, some envelopes contained no contributions and included such messages as:

* No way! They got what they asked for.
* Justice *was* done!!
* Here is my contribution to bury all traitor Jews like you. (No money enclosed)

Five years after the shooting, newspapers told of the fall of the Cambodian government of Lon Nol, the leader whom the United States supported for five years with more than one billion dollars in military aid. The students at Kent had been protesting President Nixon's Cambodian "incursion." The same newspapers called Kent State "the cataclysm, the event that once and for all turned the national consensus against the war."

Beginning May 18, 1975, the Kent State civil trial was held in Federal District Court in Cleveland, Ohio. After waiting five years to have their case heard in court, the families of the victims sat through fourteen weeks of testimony and arguments. On August 27, 1975, the jury delivered a verdict: no Ohio government officials and no Ohio National Guard officers or men were liable for the deaths and injuries suffered by students on the campus of Kent State University on May 4, 1970.

The trial was lost—or was it? Ohio officials and National Guardsmen were compelled to testify under oath. Lies, which before had been told in defense of the guard, were disclosed. Testimony supplied evidence previously withheld. The facts about the shooting have now been placed in an official record. These accounts will go a long way toward preventing another Kent

State. They also may enable the families to win their case on an appeal to a higher court.

Hanging on the wall of my office is a needlepoint by Doris Krause. It says:

ALLISON JEFF

"JUSTICE, JUSTICE SHALT THOU
FOLLOW THAT THOU MAYEST LIVE,
AND INHERIT THE LAND WHICH
THE LORD THY GOD GIVETH THEE"

DEUT. 16:20

KSU 5 4 70

BILL SANDY

When I first met Arthur Krause and Peter Davies, I was reminded of a Hebrew prophet and a colonial patriot. One was impassioned for justice, and the other was insistent about the rights of citizens. They do not now accept such tributes. They would instead point to persons who assisted them in their search for truth about Kent State, persons too numerous to list here. Yet, the words "Not Another Kent State!" have meaning today because two men would not give up and so helped save our country from despair.

10

National Conventions in Miami Beach

In the summer of 1971, the Republican and Democratic National Committees announced selected sites for their national conventions. The Democrats would meet in Miami Beach, Florida, July 10–13, 1972, and the Republicans, in San Diego, California, the following month.

These cities received the news with mixed feelings, for they remembered vividly the 1968 Democratic National Convention in Chicago. What would happen when thousands of protesters poured into Miami Beach and San Diego?

A New York *Times* article, datelined San Diego, July 24, 1971, described the reaction in that city:

> The Republican party's decision to hold its 1972 convention in San Diego was greeted today with a few cheers and considerable misgivings by the city's 700,000 citizens, most of whom have Republican loyalties.
>
> Local party officials, the Chamber of Commerce, and the Convention and Visitors Bureau talked excitedly about "putting San Diego on the map," but the reaction of others ranged from restrained enthusiasm to indifference, apprehension and anger.
>
> Even among the Republican faithful, there were many who feared what the convention might do to the city's image of order and tranquility.

Eight months later, ITT was charged with secretly pledging four hundred thousand dollars for the Republican Convention, presumably in exchange for favorable consideration in the antitrust suit being prosecuted by the United States Department of Justice. The Republican National Convention quickly relocated to Miami Beach.

Miami Beach chief of police, Rocky Pomerance, commented that if to have a political convention in one's city is to be blessed then Miami Beach was soon to be twice blessed.

The 1968 Republican National Convention had been held in Miami Beach, and the order maintained there contrasted starkly to the streets of Chicago. A confrontation across the causeway in the city of Miami, resulting in three persons' deaths in the black ghetto of Liberty City, was said to be convention-related by a study team from the National Advisory Commission on the Causes and Prevention of Violence. Since the location was a considerable distance from Convention Hall in Miami Beach, however, a comparatively favorable impression of the covention experience predominated. By late spring 1972, Miami Beach had both of the conventions and twice as much fear.

As early as July, 1971, leaders in the religious community of Greater Miami began to plan for the national political conventions of 1972. They recognized that the churches had not been prepared for the earlier confrontation in Liberty City. They also recognized that the Chicago religious community had not been able to positively influence the course of events in 1968 but, in fact, had become victims of the events.

Staff persons related to Christian Community Service, Inc., an "umbrella" under which six Protestant denominations coordinated their support of community organizations in the Greater Miami metropolitan area, called national and local religious leaders to a meeting. They hoped to create a plan by which church agencies could work toward maintaining the peace and stability of the Greater Miami community during the convention while simultaneously supporting citizens and organized groups exercising their rights of freedom of speech and assembly.

On December 6, 1971, sixteen local religious representatives gathered. I attended the meeting as a national staff person. An organization named "Religious and Community Leaders Concerned" was formed. The *concern*, of course, was for events surrounding the Democratic National Convention. Ultimately that concern was extended to include the planning for the Republican National Convention. The Steering Committee of RCLC, as it came to be known, named three coordinators—Miss Joan Gross, executive vice-president of CCSA; Rev. Jack Cassidy, minister of Metropolitan Mission of the United Church of Christ; and myself.

We worked carefully within the Religious and Community Leaders Concerned organization. I was assigned to check out national contacts and establish liaison with the convention manager of the Democratic National Committee.

I consulted with Wesley Pomeroy, now chief of police in Berkeley, California, then chairman of the Advisory Committee on Security for the Democratic National Convention. Mr. Pomeroy sent a memorandum to Richard J. Murphy, the Democratic National Convention manager, stating that he thought the involvement of the religious community in the convention planning was "a positive factor." Within a week, I met Mr. Murphy at the Watergate office building in Washington. Mr. Pomeroy also suggested an early contact with Chief Rocky Pomerance of the Miami Beach Police Department, who had been named chief of Convention Security by Governor Reuben Askew. In addition, Mr. Pomeroy arranged for four of us, representing the Steering Committee of RCLC, to meet with the Advisory Committee on Security for the Democratic National Convention, on Saturday, January 8, 1972.

Representatives of law enforcement agencies for the federal, state, and county governments and the various municipalities involved were present. Chief Pomerance listened closely to the proposed role of the religious community in the convention planning and raised several questions. Particularly, he stated his conviction that the religious community should be interested not only in "the peace and stability" of the Greater Miami area and supporting "the rights of citizens and groups to exercise fully their freedom of speech and petition," but they should also be equally concerned about the function of the political convention itself and the rights of the delegates to perform their tasks. He presented a valuable, legitimate new focus that had not been articulated previously. From that time on, the Religious and Community Leaders Concerned strove for these *three* objectives.

On February 1, 1972, RCLC staff opened an office on Lincoln Road just a block and a half from Convention Hall. Miss Gross, Rev. Cassidy, and a volunteer staff, began operating there on a daily basis. They performed their regular jobs as well as heavy additional responsibilities for RCLC.

On March 8, Religious and Community Leaders Concerned sponsored an awareness seminar to prepare the community for the conventions. Chief Pomerance, Chief Bernard Garmire of Miami, and the director of the Dade County Department of Safety, Wilson Purdy, each spoke at the day-long sessions. They said that "planning and training are self-fulfilling prophecies. If we plan openly and positively, we will have a good experience. If we plan only for violence, we will have it. We look to the total community for cooperation and support. The police share your three objectives."

Richard Murphy, the Democratic Convention manager, described the convention process and asked for citizen support. He starkly asserted that the 1972 conventions would test whether any national political conventions could be held in the future by either political party.

The Awareness Seminar legitimized RCLC work in the eyes of the "establishment." RCLC representatives were at the same time contacting leaders of the movement groups intending to come to the Democratic National Convention, including the Southern Christian Leadership Conference, the National Welfare Rights Organization, the National Tenants' Organization, and the United Farm Workers Organization.

During this period, Religious and Community Leaders Concerned focused on:

1. Orienting the general public toward citizen involvement in and support for the conventions. Besides the Awareness Seminar, several other initiatives were taken to build a stable base of support from the community.
2. Opening lines of communication with prospective protest groups,

law enforcement agencies, government offices, and the political parties.

3. Seeking legitimation of RCLC involvement from all parts of the local religious community and also from national religious groups.

We sought official endorsement of the RCLC operation by the highest levels of the National Council of Churches of Christ in the USA, the United States Catholic Conference, and the Synagogue Council of America. I contacted Dr. Cynthia Wedel, then president of the National Council of Churches, who suggested that we channel our requests through the Interreligious Committee of General Secretaries. This committee was composed of the top executives of the three major religious faiths: general secretary of the United States Catholic Conference, Bishop Joseph L. Bernardin; general secretary of the National Council of Churches, Dr. R. H. Edwin Espy; and executive vice-president of the Synagogue Council of America, Rabbi Henry Siegman.

Although not ordinarily involved in local projects, the three executives signed a letter of endorsement that said:

> We are profoundly impressed with the seriousness of your enterprise, and hope it will serve to minimize destructive conflict and to enhance the democratic process at the time of the political conventions. We believe, furthermore, that your innovative efforts can have important consequences for a wider understanding of the conciliatory role that churches and synagogues can play in the lives of men and the affairs of the nation . . . May God bless your efforts.

The Steering Committee of Religious and Community Leaders Concerned was determined to have a religiously oriented citizen presence at every possible point. Although clergymen selected by both parties would offer prayers of invocation and benediction for the sessions, RCLC was concerned that a religious presence be strategically located throughout Convention Hall, as well as on the dais. To implement this, we set up an interfaith center in a room in the Miami Beach Convention Hall. This center inside the hall could serve as a base for pastoral ministry as well as a religious-oriented communications outlet.

RCLC also suggested that the religious community furnish observers to watch the interactions among ushers responsible for Convention Hall security, delegates, representatives of the media, and police. This plan was approved by the Democratic National Convention manager and by the Andy Frain Company. RCLC carefully selected and trained an inside observer corps.

RCLC observers also would be located between the Convention Hall and the perimeter fence which circled the entire complex. Police and security personnel would be held in reserve in this area, enabling observers to relate directly with various police forces and to observe closely their actions and responses.

The largest number of volunteers would be spotted as observers on the streets and at hotel headquarters of the political parties and the various candidates. More than three hundred persons were recruited from the churches and synagogues of the Greater Miami area for this role, which took on priority responsibility during the two political conventions.

This concentration of RCLC resources in "observing" was seriously questioned by many groups. The "movement" representatives wanted to know for whom RCLC would be observing and just what it would be doing with the information it obtained. Some police representatives were cool toward having RCLC closely observe and record police actions on the streets. Many members in the religious community itself felt that "observing" was far too neutral a role for the religious community to play in such a potentially violent situation. Other people felt that the religious community should be an issue-advocate, marching with the protesters. Some believed that the churches and synagogues should primarily support the police to protect the community rather than protest with the dissenters. This deliberate strategy was not an easy decision to explain. We believed that by furnishing observers the religious community could help inhibit potentially violent types of protests, monitor the activities of the communications media, and help to avoid possible police overreaction as well as orienting a sizeable and representative segment of the local community in a disciplined way. All observers trained for twelve hours and took part in exercises which equipped them to observe as impartially, objectively, accurately, and as rapidly as possible. Movement representatives and personnel from the Miami Beach police department participated in the training.

The volunteers—Catholic, Jewish, and Protestant—became highly committed to the role. Movement leaders ultimately supported it strongly, and Chief Pomerance made certain that the twelve hundred police who would be on duty for the conventions understood the RCLC program and could readily identify the religious observer armband.

RCLC headquarters were expanded to include an operations center to which the observers reported for their shifts and to which they later reported for debriefing after assignments. Whenever possible, observers reported by telephone to a special communications center manned by RCLC volunteer operators. A daily composite was made between 4:00 A.M. and 8:00 A.M., and one copy of this report was promptly delivered to each of the movement groups, the chief of police, city manager of Miami Beach, the Community Relations Service of the United States Department of Justice, and to the Andy Frain Ushering Service.

The composite report was one additional "truthgiver," as the Andy Frain personnel often described it, or a "reality-tester," as a staff member from the Lemburg Center for the Study of Violence termed it. The composites were also meant to demonstrate that observers were functional in a specific role and not mere bystanders or curiosity seekers. The important point was that the composite reports showed that observers did not single out any segment of the convention scene for special scrutiny.

The religious community had not shaped an easy role for itself. Other groups wanted to decide what part the religious community would play. This included not only movement leaders, but also government officials and police representatives. RCLC had to say, "Let us be who we are. Let us plan as we can plan. Let us develop and maintain our institutional integrity, and we will be able to assist you far more than if we respond to your immediate demands and specific requirements."

Of course, RCLC was able to play a number of other roles. Miss Gross, Mr. Cassidy, and I were able, on the basis of the reports, to suggest to the steering committee, as well as to bishops, synodical officials, and others ways in which their offices could be used to influence what was taking place at the convention. As coordinators we acted as facilitator, expediter, and low-profile strategy-liaison. In these roles we interacted with a variety of key persons and organizations. Using a bit of organizational acrobatics, we proved that it was possible to keep the observer role impartial and objective while, at the same time, allowing coordinators to be specifically supportive of selected movement proposals, police policies, and political party plans. However, it was like walking a tightrope with no net beneath.

Probably the most vital RCLC facilitator role was obtaining a permit to use Flamingo Park as a campsite. RCLC supported the Southern Christian Leadership Conference's application for Flamingo Park. Several protest groups applied for campsites all over the city of Miami Beach, including the municipal golf course and some of the beaches.

The city council heatedly debated granting the permits and even after many meetings failed to approve a campsite. Demonstrators faced a situation similar to Chicago despite the fact that several public officials and political leaders favored approval—Mayor Chuck Hall of Miami Beach, Chief Rocky Pomerance, representatives from the Democratic National Committee, and others. As the actual date for the convention approached, Dr. Ralph David Abernathy came to Miami Beach to engage in the campsite negotiations, backing up the efforts of Ray Betts, an SCLC staff person. I telephoned Dr. Abernathy and explained the political factors at length. Although heavily scheduled, he revised his plans to attend city council meetings on June 28 and July 5. He spoke for the Poor Peoples' Coalition, which included the National Welfare Rights Organization and the National Tenants Organization, proposing that SCLC be granted the permit as an "umbrella" agency under which protest groups would be permitted to camp in Flamingo Park. The city council voted four to two on July 5 to grant the SCLC camp permit.

Since the permit applied only to the Democratic National Convention, the same process had to be replicated for the Republican

National Convention. A greater number of protesters were expected at that incumbent party's convention. Most antiwar protest groups actually bypassed the Democrats; so there was greater concern about demonstrators at the Republican National Convention.

Chief Rocky Pomerance, accused of having been irresponsibly lenient with the protesters, appeared before a Dade County grand jury investigating law enforcement in Flamingo Park during the Democratic Convention. I was called on July 27 and was able to quote the composite observer reports which described in detail the actions in the park and the various police responses.

On August 1, the grand jury issued a report to the circuit judge Harold Vann, concluding that "law enforcement was superb and regardless of what might have been alleged, the convention was a thorough success. We believe the community owes a debt of gratitude to the City of Miami Beach, the local law enforcement agencies, and to all citizens, including the non-delegates [protesters] for their mutual cooperation in creating an atmosphere conducive to peaceful demonstrations."

Discretion is one of the flexible tools of law enforcement administrators in balancing the order of the community and the rights of individuals. The grand jury report enabled negotiations for the August convention to proceed. Groups applying for campsite permits included the Peoples' Coalition for Peace and Justice, the Miami Convention's Coalition, the Miami Women's Coalition, the Youth International Party, the Effeminist Caucus, the Vietnam Veterans against the War, the National Coalition of Gay Organizations, and the Zippies who preferred to be called the Youth International Party—Zippies!

The Southern Christian Leadership Conference planned to bring only a token delegation to the second convention. This meant that a new coalition had to apply for the use of the campsite. The city manager, Chief Pomerance, and those councilmen who favored the use of the park did not believe that so-called radical organizations would be able to obtain city council approval.

On Monday, July 31, Chief Pomerance called me to suggest

that RCLC apply for the campsite permit. Rennie Davis of the Peoples' Coalition for Peace and Justice and Jeff Nightbyrd of the Youth International Party also requested that RCLC accept the coordinator role for the campsite permit. Miss Gross, Rev. Cassidy, and I met within an hour to discuss the possibility of assuming the new advocacy role. We agreed to do so if the denominational leaders approved. Checked out that afternoon, the church leaders agreed. I hand-delivered a letter to the office of the city manager, Clifford O'Key, which said that "Religious and Community Leaders Concerned not only wishes to express its strongest possible support for the granting of a permit for the campsite by the Miami Beach City Council, but it stands ready, if its services are needed, to act as the coordinator of the planning and the organizing of the campsite in cooperation with the various non-delegate groups and with the appropriate agencies of the city's government of Miami Beach."

On August 2, the council meeting adjourned without a vote. A special meeting was scheduled for August 14 to decide the issue. In the interim, RCLC representatives continued to meet with police, city officials, Republican Party representatives, and demonstration groups to work out a strategy for obtaining the campsite permit. Again, there was a long and arduous struggle before the city council finally approved the use of Flamingo Park and issued the permit to Religious and Community Leaders Concerned.

Dade County officials arranged for installation of additional electrical service, for moving in large toilet vans, for erecting large tents, and for additional trash containers throughout the camping area. A portable stage was set up in the park with an effective public address system.

Several crises occurred in Flamingo Park. One day before the opening of the Republican National Convention, the Zippies raised two flags on the public flagpole, a black flag on top and an upside-down American flag beneath. This arrangement was featured on network TV. Two hundred telephone calls to the Miami Beach Police Department denounced the desecration of the flag. One call came from as far away as Corpus Christi, Texas. Rumors of nude swimming in the Flamingo Park pool and of marijuana smoking abounded among local citizens. It looked as if the city council of Miami Beach might buckle under the pressure and revoke the permit. I met with representatives of the various protest groups in a police department training building about two blocks from the park. Each group was to send two representatives. The Zippie-SDS Coalition, however, packed the room with a large number of representatives intending to out-vote all other protest groups.

The meeting lasted for two hours. As chairman, I had to deal with innumerable interruptions, a variety of diversionary tactics, and attempted filibusters. Police officials, city representatives, and George Rodericks, director of Civil Defense in Washington, D.C., watched the progress of the meeting very closely. Finally, I had to angrily confront the leader of the Zippies. I don't recall my exact words, but I made it clear that we needed the support of every group if we were going to be able to maintain Flamingo Park as a campsite. Fortunately, at that point, a Students for a Democratic Society representative came to my rescue and spoke in support of the RCLC position. Later the flags were taken down and nude swimming discouraged. The SDS leader, a beautiful young lady who looked as if she had just come out of a church pew but who was called "leather-lungs" because of her commanding voice, later told Mr. Rodericks that she had finally supported the RCLC position in the meeting in opposition to the Zippies because "Mr. Adams sounded just like my daddy."

Perhaps we did seem paternalistic at times, but my action was calculated to counter the tactics of the Zippie leaders who seemed bent on disrupting the other protest groups and provoking the police and public officials to terminate agreements and revoke permits.

After the convention, two Chicago columnists, Jack Mabley and Mike Royko, reported their suspicions that the Zippies were recruited, organized, and funded to create confusion and produce violence at the Republican National Convention. Royko asked, "Is anybody in the White House the real leader of the Zippies? . . . A few months ago this suspicion might have been laughed off. But now we've had burglaries, buggings, Maurice Stans' mysterious financing, White House aides in cloak-and-dagger roles, ex-FBI men swearing that they were in on political espionage, poison pen leaders and other mischief."[1]

Mabley was more direct: "Until I see evidence to the contrary, I am satisfied that the street rioting was a deliberate, well-financed plot to sabotage the anti-war protests in Miami Beach, and to simultaneously discredit McGovern and the Democrats. Circumstantial evidence gives every reason to believe the Republicans who financed the Watergate episode were involved."[2]

Religious and Community Leaders Concerned assumed at both conventions that informers, spies, and provocatures infiltrated the group even though they could not be identified. We observed erratic actions and very mysterious turns of events. It became obvious that RCLC personnel in strategic places deterred "dirty tricks" and reduced the number of potentially violent confrontations. Whoever planned the activities of the Zippies clearly underestimated the highly organized and wide-ranging involvements of Religious and Community Leaders Concerned.

Insubordinate actions by segments of the interdepartmental police force also occurred. Most took place on the last night of the Republican Convention. Early in the evening certain police units were authorized to use tear gas to control small groups of protesters led by Zippies who were attacking automobiles and buses and assaulting delegates as they arrived at Convention Hall. After controlling that situation, many police continued to fire tear gas at peacefully protesting groups, in failing to distinguish between the lawful and the unlawful. The most outrageous police action occurred at the campsite. At approximately 9:00 P.M., a contingent of Miami police hurled tear gas canisters into the park and systematically smashed the headlights of automobiles and motorcycles belonging to protesters. Three public employees from Flamingo Park, including a plainclothes Miami Beach policeman, appealed to the policemen to respect the park as a refuge and leave the area. Cursing and threatening to come back and take care of public officials as well as protesters, the police left.

1. Chicago *Daily News*, October 18, 1972.
2. *Chicago Today*, October 26, 1972.

At 12:20 A.M., after the convention had ended, thirty Miami police reentered the park, chasing young people. Police cars and motorcycles then closely circled the park. Tension mounted. Many campers snatched rocks, sticks, and any weapon at hand to throw at the patrol cars. One public official phoned the Communications Center, asking me to come to the park. A major confrontation was imminent. When I saw the situation for myself, I called the police command post and requested the removal of the police from the area, at least temporarily. I was told that no police were authorized in the area and that, in fact, the police dispatcher reported that none were near the park. I requested barricades at intersections surrounding the park in order to stop the flow of traffic, including the patrol cars. Two Miami Beach scout cars arrived within ten minutes; the streets were closed to traffic, and the confrontation ended.

I spent the next half-hour walking the streets next to the park and asking young people to put down their improvised weapons and go back to their tents and shanties and try to get some sleep. Although the air was still heavy with tear gas, their own security personnel helped quiet the scene, and there was little resistance. I picked up a few "weapons" which they left behind and threw them into the back of squad cars parked near a barricade. When the camp was finally secure, it was after 3:30 A.M. Within five or six hours, the campers were packing up and moving out.

Despite problems, there was a surprising degree of trust between police officials and most protest leaders throughout the conventions. There was often real and essential cooperation behind the scenes. Without this level of cooperation the protest groups literally would have collided with one another as they tried to make their appearances and demonstrate their issues on the streets outside the Convention Hall. Chief Pomerance and his assistants planned carefully with each group, setting alternate routes, establishing times at which the different marches would begin, and estimating the times of arrival at the hall. The whole scene had to be orchestrated and required the closest possible coordination between law enforcement units and movement leaders.

Clearly, Chief Pomerance deserves credit for the atmosphere of openness and cooperation. He was available to protest leaders early in the spring of 1972 and remained accessible through the close of the conventions. Frequently he gave assistance to protest groups, and yet he never compromised his position as a law enforcement administrator. Chief Pomerance was respected precisely for what he was—a policeman.

During the 1972 political conventions the religious community learned that it does not always have to be an activist or an advocate in crisis situations. Sometimes all that is required is to be present and to be identified as "impartial observers" to prevent useless confrontations.

When planning begins early enough, when lines of communication are adequately opened, and when the rights of all persons are given sufficient consideration both by those in power and those challenging public policy, there can be peaceful and effective protest.

11

Wounded Knee

On the night of February 27, 1973, a caravan of armed Indians occupied Wounded Knee, South Dakota, on the Pine Ridge Reservation of the Oglala Sioux. Two churches, a trading post and museum, and two private homes were taken over by armed force in protest against policies of the Bureau of Indian Affairs and what was considered maladministration of the tribal chairman. The national leadership of the American Indian Movement strongly supported local Indians involved in the action.

Federal Bureau of Investigation agents and Bureau of Indian Affairs police immediately sealed off every road leading out of the village. Shots were exchanged, and a seige lasting seventy-one days began.

The federal government sent out its Special Operations Group, an elite, volunteer, highly trained strike force from the United States marshals which is only assigned by order of the president or the attorney general of the United States. FBI agents throughout the country were brought in on special assignment. Additional BIA police were transferred to Pine Ridge from other reservations. Armored personnel carriers were trucked to the federal roadblocks. The mobilization was intended to neutralize the armed occupiers of Wounded Knee and then either force them to surrender or stage an armed assault in which they would be captured. Not only were law enforcement personnel dispatched to the scene, but large amounts of military equipment were moved into the area. The seriousness with which the government countered the armed Indians in the Wounded Knee district is indicated by a document later submitted by the government in a trial in St. Paul. One inventory list of material assigned by the Department of Defense to the Department of Justice on the Pine Ridge Reservation included:

50,000 rounds M-16 ammunition
11,760 rounds M-16 tracer ammo
8,200 rounds M-1 ball ammo
2,500 star parachute flares
20 sniper rifles
M-79 grenade launchers
6 quarter ton trucks
1—400 gallon water trailer
combat rations, mine detectors, helmets, field telephones, ammunition pouches, search lights, mountain stoves, folding cots, air mattresses, ponchos, parkas, arctic boots, and mittens with trigger fingers.

News of the dangerous confrontation and imminent assault was reported to the governing board of the National Council of Churches in session in Pittsburgh, Pennsylvania. The board authorized the following telegram to the president of the United States, the United States attorney general, the governor of South Dakota, the South Dakota attorney general, the South Dakota congressional delegation, the tribal chairman of the Pine Ridge Reservation, and the director of the Bureau of Indian Affairs:

> The existing crisis at Wounded Knee, S.D. brings into sharp focus our awareness of the violation of our intra-national treaties for which we all share responsibility. As Christians, we are compelled to express our deep concern that this current conflict be resolved through sympathetic negotiation with those who are aggrieved.
>
> The massacre of Wounded Knee in 1890 is a sad chapter in American history. We as followers of the Christ abhor such acts of vio-

> lence against innocent people. Churches, through their historical inability to respond to the continuing deep human hurts of American Indians, are partners in the creation of the crisis which is now before us. Our Lord and Savior calls up to reconciliation through justice, but the "Trail of Broken Treaties" has highlighted the level at which injustices toward the Native American people continue.
>
> Therefore, I am authorized by our Governing Board now meeting in Pittsburgh, to call upon you to exercise your good offices in bringing to a speedy conclusion a peaceful settlement of this situation.

The board also authorized the president of the NCC, Dr. W. Sterling Carey, to name someone to deliver personally the communication "to all those involved in the situation at Wounded Knee with the understanding that such person remain as long as seems useful as our personal emissary seeking to implement the spirit and concern." Dr. Carey named James Armstrong, bishop of the Dakotas area of the United Methodist church, to go to Pine Ridge. Bishop Armstrong asked me to come and remain on the reservation as his representative.

I arrived in Pine Ridge late Friday, March 2, 1973. John Terronez, a Community Relations Service field representative, agreed to take me through the federal road block on Big Foot Trail.

After we proceeded a hundred yards beyond the roadblock, he stopped his car, climbed out, and tied his white handkerchief to the radio antenna to signal our neutrality as we approached the Indian roadblock a mile and a half ahead. At the roadblock, three Indian young men signaled us to stop, cautiously coming from behind a burned-out truck which blocked the road. They checked our identification. After I explained that I represented the National Council of Churches and was following up on Bishop Armstrong's visit that afternoon, they allowed me to pass. I met with Vernon Long, Pedro Bissonette, and other officers of the Oglala Sioux Civil Rights Organization as well as Dennis Banks, Russell Means, Clyde Bellecourt, Carter Camp, national leaders of the American Indian Movement. They asked whether I intended to stay in Wounded Knee with them as Dr. Paul Boe had done. An executive from the American Lutheran church, Dr. Boe had come from Minneapolis and lived inside the occupied area for nearly a week.

I explained that the NCC hoped to prevent bloodshed and to help in any responsible way in finding a peaceful resolution to the confrontation. We could probably do that better, I continued, if all bases were covered and I did not stay inside.

Local leaders and AIM representatives declared that they stood ready to die and that the occupation would continue until some high-level official in Washington came to Wounded Knee to engage in good-faith discussions about treaty rights and take action on problems endemic to the Pine Ridge Reservation specifically. They believed that the government wanted only to negotiate the disarming and arrest of those inside Wounded Knee. Otherwise, government forces would move in and wipe them out. They expressed concern for the permanent residents trapped inside. Families were running short of food and other necessities. A number of persons had become sick in the bitter cold and needed medical attention. The leaders asked us to work on those problems and to try to persuade the government to allow one telephone so that they could talk with lawyers. I promised to check out these matters and return the next day.

Rev. and Mrs. George Pierce invited us to stay in the rectory of the Episcopal Church of the Holy Cross in Pine Ridge. The Pierces, missionaries to the Sioux for years, were intimately acquainted with Indian families throughout the reservation. We talked late that first night. The Pierces described the complexities of the local issues and made clear the dangers which would accompany any involvement of the National Council of Churches. They were ready to support us, however. The Church of the Holy Cross and their home became the center of NCC activity for three weeks, which under the conditions was a singular act of courage.

We were told the next morning that the Department of Justice was effecting a policy of restraint, but it was an apparent impatient restraint which soon would wear out unless a surrender took place rapidly. They did not want bloodshed, but they wanted the occupation ended promptly. There would be no negotiations on issues other than disarmament and arrests. Washington was not going to negotiate under the gun. However, food and medical problems were taken under consideration, and the telephone was a possibility. NCC representatives were cleared to move through the federal roadblock (RB-1) freely.

Pine Ridge was tense and quiet. In the center of the dusty main intersection, an oil drum stood with posters plastered on it announcing the free movie of the week, "Killers Three." Indians walked around town but didn't seem to be going anywhere, just trying to stay out of the way of something. Only FBI agents in camouflaged combat fatigues, United States marshals in bright blue jumpsuits, and casually dressed reporters moved in deliberate directions. The agents and marshals rotated shifts at the roadblocks. Reporters gleaned out the last news release and tried to anticipate the next action.

Everyone expected an assault order from Washington. Wounded Knee was eighteen miles away, but any sweep of that area would immediately send shock waves into Pine Ridge. Almost every family in Pine Ridge had relatives in Wounded Knee, both among the residents and the dissidents.

Even though the Indians inside Wounded Knee had far fewer guns than did the marshals and agents on the nearby hills, and those they had were of smaller caliber and of lesser fire power, I came to realize that they had a weapon more powerful than any the government could ship to Pine Ridge. They possessed the site where Chief Big Foot's band had been massacred on December 29, 1890, and they were now custodians of the mass burial grave.

Wounded Knee, 1890

After U.S. Indian Service Police killed Chief Sitting Bull at Standing Rock on December 15, 1890, the remaining chiefs believed that they and their followers would be the next targets. Chief Big Foot, old and sick with pneumonia, decided to surrender, but he wanted to lead his band of Minneconjou Sioux to Pine Ridge where they could give up under the protection of the influential Oglala chief, Red Cloud. However, scouts of the United States Seventh Cavalry interpreted the movement as aggressive action. Four troops of soldiers were dispatched to intercept the 350 men, women, and children straggling toward the Pine Ridge agency.

As the troops approached the Sioux, Big Foot sent out a representative under a white flag to ask for a parley. The request was rejected and unconditional surrender demanded. Big Foot surrendered. The troops moved the Minneconjou to an encampment at Wounded Knee Creek where they remained overnight.

Additional troops and two Hotchkiss guns, capable of firing fifty two-pound explosive shells per minute, were sent out from Pine Ridge, seventeen miles away. Finally, 470 Cavalrymen surrounded the 106 warriors, women, and children; pieces of deadly artillery were positioned on a hill fifty yards above the Indian camp, aimed precisely at their tepees.[1]

Indians slept anxiously under the gun the night of December 28, 1890. The commander had delayed the disarming of the Indians until reveille the next morning. At exactly 8:00 A.M. on Sunday, December 29, Colonel Forsyth, the commander of the troops, ordered the Indians out of their tents, demanding their guns. Thirty weapons were confiscated. In a further search, one Indian, whom his tribesmen later claimed was deaf, refused to give up his new Winchester, and it discharged as it was wrestled from him. That one shot triggered a heavy blanket of gunfire from the Seventh Cavalry troops.

Dee Brown, the historian, describes it: "In the first seconds of violence, the firing of carbines was deafening, filling the air with powder smoke. Among the dying who lay sprawled on the frozen ground was Big Foot. Then there was a brief lull in the rattle of arms, with small groups of Indians and soldiers grappling at close quarters, using knives, clubs, and pistols. As few of the Indians had arms, they soon had to flee, and then the big Hotchkiss guns on the hill opened up on them, firing almost a shell a second, raking the Indian camp, shredding the tepees with flying shrapnel, killing men, women, and children."[2]

The few warriors left, together with women and children, ran

1. Will H. Spindler, *Tragedy Strikes at Wounded Knee* (Vermillion, South Dakota: University of South Dakota Press, 1972), p. 21.

2. Dee Brown, *Bury My Heart at Wounded Knee* (New York: Holt, Rinehart, Winston, 1971), p. 444.

up the ravine and into the gullies. Soldiers on horseback pursued them, firing as they huddled against the dirt banks for protection. When the gunfire ended, more than two hundred fifty Indians were dead and twenty-five soldiers had lost their lives, most of them hit by bullets and shrapnel from the Seventh Cavalry guns.

Open-bed wagons carried the wounded Indians, four men and forty-seven women and children, to Pine Ridge. After much delay an emergency aid station was set up in the Episcopal Mission, where the pews were removed and the injured laid on the rough floor. The dead Indians left at Wounded Knee were to be picked up later. Three days after the engagement, the bodies, frozen into grotesque shapes by heavy subzero snow storms, were loaded onto wagons, carried to the top of the hill where the Hotchkiss guns had been located, and buried in a single long trench.

The report of James Mooney, whom the Bureau of Ethnology sent to investigate the clash, stated, "There can be no question that the pursuit was simply a massacre, where fleeing women, some with infants in their arms, were shot down after resistance had ceased and when almost every warrior was stretched dead or dying on the ground."[3]

The fact that many of the troops had once served under General George A. Custer when 274 troopers of the Seventh Cavalry had been wiped out in Montana on June 25, 1876, might account for their ferociousness. Wounded Knee was revenge for Little Big Horn.[4]

On June 25, 1891, six months after Wounded Knee and the fifteenth anniversary of the defeat of the Seventh Cavalry at Little Big Horn, Congressional Medals of Honor were awarded to eighteen troopers for the role that they had played at Wounded Knee.[5]

Wounded Knee, 1973

The signs along the road said in immense letters, "Wounded Knee Massacre Site—Mass Grave—Museum." The official South

3. Spindler, *Tragedy Strikes at Wounded Knee*, p. 25.
4. Ibid., p. 23.
5. Ibid., p. 28.

Dakota map, marked with a red X, designated the "Battle of Wounded Knee." The roadside signs and the South Dakota map hinted at differing historical interpretations. Whites called it a battle; Indians, a massacre.

Nevertheless, by 1973, there had been more than thirty printings of Dee Brown's book, *Bury My Heart at Wounded Knee.* Hundreds of thousands of white persons had read the book and knew that Wounded Knee stood for injustice. There had been a *massacre* there.

Every square foot of ground inside Wounded Knee was mined, not with explosives, but with political sympathy. News reporters, not only from every part of the United States, but literally from over the entire world, came to Wounded Knee. National television networks parked vans within the Wounded Knee district so that their representatives could live within the occupied area and cover the events from day to day within the battle zone. Paperback copies of *Bury My Heart at Wounded Knee* stuck out of their back pockets. They read about the 1890 massacre during the lulls in the 1973 confrontation.

A Harris Poll, taken shortly after the occupation began, reported that:

> 93% of the public was following the episode at Wounded Knee.
> 75% of those polled believed that Indians had not been treated well in this country.
> 60% of those questioned supported the major claims of the Indians at Wounded Knee.

Vine Deloria, Jr., had written back in 1969, ". . . the general public has sat back, shed tears over the treatment of Indians a century ago, and bemoaned the plight of the Indian. In many instances, when the tribes have attempted to bring their case before the public, it has turned a deaf ear, claiming that the treaties are some historical fancy dreamed up by the Indian to justify his irresponsbility."[6]

The American people tend to deplore cruelties toward Indians

6. Vine Deloria, Jr., *Custer Died for Your Sins* (New York: Avon, 1969), p. 47.

in another age while disbelieving injustices of the present. Wounded Knee, 1973, invited the usual romanticizing about Indians. Until the event gained the public's attention, the treaty rights issue was a matter which the government and most white Americans felt had been disposed of a hundred years ago.

White people, who had read about the ruthlessness of the Seventh Cavalry in 1890, were suddenly faced with the reality of present-day injustices toward native Americans, rooted in the violation of treaties once solemnly signed by representatives of the United States government and ratified by Congress.

It was not always clear from the government's strategy whether its representatives in Pine Ridge understood the social and political impact which might result from a full-scale assault on the Wounded Knee massacre site.

There were many government strategies because many government agencies were involved. The Department of Justice was in charge of the Pine Ridge operation, but a steady rotation of assistant attorneys general acted as negotiators. Also involved were the Federal Bureau of Investigation, United States marshals, and the Community Relations Service, all from the Department of Justice. The Department of Interior was well represented by personnel directly from Washington; Bureau of Indian Affairs supervisors and superintendents were ever present.

Sometimes the marshals would take one tack; the FBI another. One assistant attorney general would take a hard line and issue ultimatums; the next would be open and flexible and seek good-faith negotiations. Often their assistants would privately negate their strategy and countermand their orders.

The tribal council chairman, Richard Wilson, would at times oppose the government course. He did threaten to launch his own assault on those who occupied the village and said he had eight hundred to nine hundred armed men waiting to participate in the assault. He favored an assault on those who occupied Wounded Knee for he saw it as a law enforcement issue. The men he had waiting were white ranchers who leased reservation lands for cattle grazing.

The picture was complex, confused, and dangerous. We became convinced that the church needed to support a negotiational posture on the part of the government. An assault would inevitably lead to the loss of many lives, and those lives would have been Indian since the government had superior fire power, armored personnel carriers, and other protective equipment.

An assault would lead to a 1973 massacre on the 1890 massacre site. The repercussions, immediate and violent on reservations and in cities, would have been like the death and destruction that set the country ablaze after the assassination of Dr. Martin Luther King, Jr. Those who pressed for an assault did not realize that. They seemed insensitive to the impact on other reservations and urban areas.

Those within the government working for a peaceful settlement —and there were many—were caught in a political crossfire. The tribal chairman, who had called in the Department of Justice to enforce the law suggested that nothing could be gained from negotiation and that assault was the only solution.

Watergate was about to burst, and the pressure within the Department of Justice was enormous. Justice Department personnel were needed back in Washington to help plug the dikes, thus the steady turnover in justice officials. Pressure for a quick solution had a negative effect. Later, Watergate helped those in Wounded Knee, for the administration realized that it could not endure an Indian massacre and the public outcry which it would evoke, while dealing with the coverup exposures.

Some agents and marshals on the federal perimeter were impatient. Their assignment to Wounded Knee was different from those to which they were ordinarily assigned. They wanted to get it over with and couldn't understand the delay.

Inside Wounded Knee, Indian leaders had their own problems in maintaining support for negotiations. Some wanted to "get it on" and demanded more aggressive action. The bitter cold winds, the long tense hours in the bunkers, the lack of cold-weather equipment, inadequate food—all these elements brought great pressures upon the Indian leaders from their followers. Extraordinary discipline was required to hold back the frustrated who wanted to shoot it out. They had had enough. They were ready to be buried at Wounded Knee.

For the first week, we of the NCC worked twenty to twenty-two hours a day. Most government contacts had to be made in the daytime; long consultations with the Indians usually took place at night. In between, we reported by telephone to Bishop Armstrong in Aberdeen, the NCC officials in New York, exchanged information with officials and staff aides in Washington, and tried to return a barrage of telephone calls from concerned organizations and individuals all over the country.

Our meals consisted mainly of fruit and sandwiches, eaten as we drove back and forth between the BIA building in Pine Ridge (the federal command post) and Wounded Knee. We endeavored to keep in constant touch with an array of federal officials while developing lines of trust and opening channels of communication with leaders of the American Indian Movement and officers of the Oglala Sioux Civil Rights Organization.

We were racing violence. As representatives of national religious organizations, we had no power, but we could furnish a presence, and we kept shuttling it between the two sides. We gained an advantage by working more hours than others—while Indians slept during the day and government officials at night, we circulated. Tentatively but adequately, our liaison was accepted and trusted by both government representatives and Indian leaders.

Moving between the lines, we watched a phenomenon which psychiatrists call "object-dehumanization," a process in which individuals and groups of persons treat one another ultimately as bad-humans or nonpersons. It becomes possible to withhold from the dehumanized individuals or groups the restraints which would be exercised toward human beings. It is the necessary metamorphosis which precedes murder.

Many FBI agents and U.S. marshals described the Indians inside Wounded Knee as "savages" and "criminals." The Indians on security detail in the occupied area spoke of the agents and marshals as "pigs."

We knew that we had to do everything we could to counteract

the dehumanizing process and deliberately reported to government officials what *Mr.* Banks had said or what *Mr.* Bissonette had suggested. We similarly referred to the government personnel by their titles when we spoke with the Indians. Also we never missed an opportunity to describe the human factors we had observed in dealing with the other side.

We considered this a religious witness—a very practical and necessary one. Jesus said, "Pray for your enemies." He taught that when you pray for someone you consider that person a human being created by God. To pray for one's enemy is to humanize him; then the restraints are restored. This does not mean that all differences are resolved; it simply provides an opportunity for new understanding and possible agreement.

In our liaison role we transported limited quantities of food and other supplies into the occupied area. In order to allay concern that we might transport guns, ammunition, or any other contraband into Wounded Knee, we agreed that the food, which was furnished by the National Council of Churches, would be inspected by a United States marshal, packed in NCC vehicles in his presence, and then be escorted into Wounded Knee by representatives of the Community Relations Service.

Father George Pierce and Sister Margaret Hawk of the Episcopal Mission, who knew the resident families in Wounded Knee, accompanied the shipments and participated in the distribution. Later we were also permitted to take food directly to the commissary set up in the former trading post.

While delivering supplies and working to meet some of the human needs, we could also monitor moods, check perceptions, and pick up clues that would help us keep alive every opportunity for negotiation. During the first week this was particularly important, for the government's position was rather rigid and the temper within Wounded Knee was grim.

One night, inside the occupied area, morale was low, and the Indians seemed dangerously isolated. They asked me to contact Dr. Ralph Abernathy and extend an invitation from the AIM leadership to come to Wounded Knee.

Within forty-eight hours Dr. Abernathy was in Pine Ridge. I

had to obtain clearance from Washington for him to pass through the federal roadblock. It was given on the condition that an assistant attorney general would brief Dr. Abernathy before we headed out Big Foot Trail.

We cleared the roadblock and proceeded toward the AIM security point. "Do you think they will hold me hostage?" Dr. Abernathy asked with a thin smile. "I hear," he said, "that some black soldiers fought against the Indians a hundred years ago and that there are still bitter memories about it." (The Ninth Cavalry was composed of black troops and served in the area.)

"Dr. Abernathy," I replied, "if they haven't taken me hostage, they won't take you. You've been invited."

Arriving in Wounded Knee, we were taken to a tepee which had been set up for the occasion. The protest leaders were waiting for us. A brilliant fire burned in the center of the tent. A peace pipe leaned against a buffalo skull which was set on a bear skin at the head of the circle. Dr. Abernathy was directed to a place of honor. The pipe was passed, and a long relaxed exchange of thoughts began. The Indians explained the issues related to the treaties and the critical stage which had been reached in the efforts to negotiate.

Dr. Abernathy responded to the whole community by saying:

> As I have come to this place—making this pilgrimage to Wounded Knee—and turning my thoughts to those who were slain here—I think of Dr. Martin Luther King, Jr., of whom I was a close companion as he walked and talked, as he marched and prayed in the struggle to gain the civil rights of the black people of this nation. Yet I know that he marched not only for blacks—but for Indians, Mexican Americans, Puerto Ricans, and others who have suffered the neglects and injustices which have been perpetrated by this rich and affluent nation . . . Dr. King gave his life for his people—and I think for all people. Without violence he confronted this nation, this society, this government—until they knew that the time had come for this country to live up to its grand declarations.
>
> There is a memorial in Atlanta, Georgia, to Dr. Martin Luther King, Jr. His tomb is near to where he grew up and where he worked. It is a sacred site to black people. I come from that place—to this

> place. I have made a pilgrimage from the tomb of Dr. Martin Luther King, Jr., to Wounded Knee. This is a great symbol, I believe. It ought to express to the American people that two great peoples who have suffered separately in the past—are committed to seeking justice together in the future.

As we left Wounded Knee later that night, I noticed one young man after another—with a gun in one hand—reaching out with the other just to touch a black Baptist minister who is an exponent of nonviolent social change.

Dr. Abernathy's coming was important, for only hours before his arrival the government had suddenly issued an ultimatum, part of which spoke for itself:

> In view of the dangerous situation brought about by the breakdown in negotiations with the nonresidents, residents are urged to leave Wounded Knee if possible, or at least to send their women and children out until the present situation is ended. For their own safety the women and children should leave by 6 P.M., Thursday.

In Wounded Knee it was believed that the end was coming the next day and that it would be violent.

12

Is There Anything We Can Do to Avoid Violence?

As we left the village, I sensed a feeling of finality, not only about the night, but for a community of people who were in grave danger. Undercover agents inside Wounded Knee may have advised the government that an ultimatum would tip and then topple the leadership of the occupation. I knew that not to be true; too many inside had pledged to die if necessary, and many of them were teenagers. Some were children of tribal officials.

How could we prevent another Kent State, Jackson State—or Attica? I went to bed, but late as it was, I could not sleep. I don't know whether I was worrying or praying. Questions kept tripping my mind. Is there anything we can do to avoid violence? There were no answers. Maybe something could be done in the morning; no, it already was morning, nearly daybreak. I did pray then, specifically asking for guidance. I got up and went down to Father Pierce's office in the basement of the rectory and started typing. Within an hour and a half I had written a fifteen-point proposal to the Oglala Sioux Civil Rights Organization, the American Indian Movement, and the United States Department of Justice. It began:

> In consideration of the extremely delicate and dangerous situation which has been created in Wounded Knee, South Dakota, because of

the rupture in negotiations between the United States Department of Justice and the United States Department of Interior, on the one hand, and the residents of the Wounded Knee District of the Pine Ridge Reservation and the leaders of the American Indian Movement on the other:

The National Council of Churches of Christ in the U.S.A. working through its designated representatives who are on the scene at Wounded Knee, PROPOSES to the American Indian Movement and the United States Department of Justice the following steps to be effected:

1. A cease-fire be ordered by the security forces of both the American Indian Movement and the United States Department of Justice, beginning at 5 PM on Thursday, March 8, 1973, and that the cease-fire remain in effect indefinitely.

Fourteen points followed. One of them authorized the NCC to furnish observers in strategic locations in a demilitarized zone, under the supervision of the Community Relations Service. Another provided for a staged withdrawal of weapons in preparation for negotiations on the substantive issues.

It wasn't a refined document, but it was worth testing out. I called NCC officials at their homes in New York, and they gave me permission to present the agreement as an official NCC proposal. I checked with Bishop Armstrong in Aberdeen, and he immediately arranged a charter flight to Pine Ridge in order to help get an agreement before the deadline. I next telephoned my liaison contact with the Department of Justice in Washington who listened closely as I read the fifteen points. He thought they were useful. "Repeat them slowly," he said. "I am going to tape the proposal. I will have it on the attorney general's desk within an hour. Call me back in three hours, and I will give you a reply."

When the bishop's plane landed at the Pine Ridge airport, I had the fifteen points spread across the front seat of my car. He read them as I drove directly to Wounded Knee. Driving out Big Foot Trail, we observed additional armored personnel carriers and other heavy equipment being moved into place. There were more agents and marshals on duty. Security had tightened at the federal roadblock. We received cold stares and only reluctant clearance to enter the occupied area.

When we arrived in the village, we asked the leadership to gather for an immediate meeting. As they filed into the little house, we gave them copies of the proposal. They crowded onto the couch and the three or four chairs and began reading.

"We'll go with it," Russell Means said.

"It's workable," Dennis Banks agreed, and all the others expressed support.

Bishop Armstrong interpreted the status of the document, saying that we were going back into Pine Ridge to check the reception the proposal was getting from government officials at the BIA building. Rev. Wesley Hunter, executive secretary of the Association of Christian Churches of South Dakota, had delivered copies to them while we were in Wounded Knee.

I stopped off at the rectory and called my Washington contact. "The reaction is favorable here," he told me. "They were ready for anything positive. They had gotten themselves in a box. They didn't have anything else; so it looks as if they are going with what you have proposed."

"When will that word get to officials out here?" I asked.

"It should be coming through soon," my friend assured me.

The bishop, two other NCC representatives, and I cooled our collars for hours in an office in the BIA building, waiting for the word from Washington to be shaped into a revised policy in Pine Ridge. We watched Justice and Interior personnel scurry from one meeting to another, but there was still no word as late afternoon approached. We began to wonder whether the assessment I had received from Washington was accurate. Nothing seemed to be changing in Pine Ridge. Then, at literally the last minute, an announcement was made by a Justice Department official. The NCC document was accepted as a working document; there was a cease-fire; negotiations would be resumed.

The next day negotiations were arranged between the federal and Indian roadblocks in a demilitarized zone. National Council observers were assigned. However, within twenty-six hours, without any notice, heavy firing was triggered between the defense perimeters of the two forces.

It was night. I had just finished attending a meeting at which leaders of AIM and their lawyers had reviewed the negotiations and political maneuvers of the day. Russell Means, an AIM leader, and I went to the phone in the trading post to talk to a medical doctor who had offered to volunteer for duty in the small village. A heavy exchange of gunfire took place.

Mr. Means signaled for lights out, calling all security personnel to go outside and await instructions. Since I was at Mr. Means's side, he said, "Come with me," and I followed him outside the building.

As soon as we walked into the darkness, a young man ran up and exclaimed, "They fired at us first, Russ."

Mr. Means said, "Continue to return the fire."

Seeing—and hearing—what was happening, I said in as few words as possible, "Russ, I have to get up to the federal roadblock. Can I drive my car?"

He answered, "Yes, but you can't turn on your lights until you're over that hill. Here, two of you," he said, speaking to the security personnel huddled near him, "run alongside his car until he's over that rise."

I backed the car in the darkness and began to drive up the road, watching out for the young men who were visible on either side of the car. I drove slowly until I got over the hill, then switched on the lights and sped toward the federal roadblock. I pulled within twenty-five yards of the armored personnel carrier and agents' cars blocking the road. A blinding blue strobe light beamed onto the windshield; I could barely see the three officers who charged my car.

"We're under fire! Turn off your lights!" they shouted. "Don't move." I didn't, but when they got to the car window, I explained that the shooting was the reason I was there. I asked to see the agent in charge. It took minutes, which seemed like hours, to be cleared through the narrow opening between the vehicles—a movement understandably unappreciated at that time by some of the men at the roadblock. But under the circumstances, it had to be done.

I spoke to the agent in charge by name and said, "They say down there that you started the firing."

He replied, "Reverend, I just got confirmed reports. They started the exchange!"

"All right, how can it be stopped?" I asked.

"We will stop firing when they stop firing," he stated simply.

"Okay, can I turn around and drive back down?"

"Yes, but don't turn on your lights for fifty yards."

Agents guided me as I turned the car around on the narrow road which had deep ditches on either side. I drove off, imagining the center of the road for the first fifty yards. Then, turning on the lights, I jammed my foot down on the gas pedal. As I neared the village, I flicked the headlights of the car on and off, turning them off entirely as I neared the trading post.

Mr. Means was nearby. I got out of the car, rushed to him, and said, "They said you fired first, Russ."

"Dammit, John, I just got another report. They started it!"

"Okay," I said, "but they will stop firing when you do. Will you pull back your men in that one sector?"

He stood in the middle of a group of armed Indians, looked away for a moment, and said, "All right, we will!"

"I must get back up there then. Can I turn my car around and take off again?"

He said yes, and they helped me turn the car around in the dark. As two men ran alongside, I drove off. Once over the little hill, I raced the distance to the federal roadblock. This time agents shouted, "You idiot!" Privately I agreed with them. They continued shouting, "You come up here one more time and you're going to get shot!"

They rushed the car and thrust guns through the rolled-down window. I explained rapidly: "I have to see the special agent in charge again. It's important."

One of the agents commented, "We're not out here for our health, you know."

I had been signaled ahead, and as the car was beginning to move, I replied, "Neither am I, and I don't even have a gun."

When I finally edged the automobile between the armored vehicles to reach the special agent in charge, I said, "They are pulling their men back over there. Will you signal a cease-fire?"

"I will," he replied. He immediately crawled into the armored personnel carrier and, in my presence, picked up the microphone ordering a cease-fire. Instantly it was quiet. The next morning in a federal debriefing I heard the chief of the United States marshals confirm the fact that the exchange of gunfire was initiated by shots from neither the government forces nor the Indians inside Wounded Knee. The shots came from the right and to the rear of federal roadblock number one. The government had information that a vigilante force had fired into Wounded Knee in order to trigger a shoot-out between the government and the Indian security forces.

I then understood a little more clearly how some wars start and how they perpetuate themselves. I also became convinced that at times a person has to fight for nonviolence. I remembered the words of Dietrich Bonhoeffer in *Prisoner for God*: "There's a kind of weakness Christianity will not stand for, but which everyone seems to expect Christianity to tolerate." The NCC view at Wounded Knee was that the guns represented weakness, not strength, and that their use could not be tolerated. We endeavored to stand between them until the investment in negotiations was great enough that both sides would continue.

After the shooting, during the hours of the night, the government reassessed the total situation and concluded that it would be useful for all federal forces to be removed. The withdrawal of the federal personnel might produce a nonconflict, and those occupying Wounded Knee would realize that there was no percentage to be gained in remaining in the village. Early Saturday morning a negotiating session was held in a military bus parked in the demilitarized zone. I sat in the back of the bus, listening to the chief of the United States Marshal Service and the chief of security for the Indian forces at Wounded Knee negotiate. It was like a game of chess in which the two players agreed on a strategy and a sequence by which each other's pieces would be removed from the board. The chief of the marshals would say, "You dismantle your bunkers here, and I will remove my armored personnel carriers there. You take this down and I will pull this back." As a result, by noon Saturday, March 10, 1973, all roads to Wounded Knee were open, and the people flooded in for a great victory celebration.

Federal forces were removed, and Indian fortifications dismantled. I decided to attend a meeting of families of the victims of the Kent State shooting which had been scheduled in Cleveland, Ohio, for the next day, March 11, for several months. I also needed to take Rev. Wesley Hunter, who had physically collapsed from exhaustion, to Rapid City. In my presence he had actually fallen over as a result of near-pneumonia and extreme fatigue. We had all worked too many hours and had been overexposed to high winds and bitter cold. At Rapid City a charter plane took Mr. Hunter home to Huron where he was hospitalized.

Agents assigned to assess damages and gather evidence for a grand jury came into Wounded Knee, creating a new tense situation.

I went on to Cleveland, attended the meeting, and immediately returned to Wounded Knee. There had been a shoot-out between two FBI agents and some Indians driving a camouflaged van. The shoot-out provoked another conflict. Within hours federal forces were back on the perimeter, and Indians were manning new fortifications.

Immediately upon arriving, I made my way through the roadblocks to consult with the Indians. I intended to return to federal officials and recheck all signals about reengaging in negotiations. I had some difficulty getting through the AIM roadblock. My pass was questioned. When I finally got into the center of the occupied community, I was ostracized. It was like walking into a social deep-freeze. None of the leaders—none of the people—would even speak to me. I eventually stopped Dennis Banks and told him that I needed to talk with him, but he said he didn't want to talk with me. "Well, in that case," I said, "that's even more reason that I *have* to talk with you."

Finally, he took me into one of the houses the Indians had confiscated, and we began talking. I asked what was wrong. He was silent. Moments later he said, "When you left, it all came down on us. Some people here are convinced that you work for the FBI."

I replied that the FBI was simultaneously saying that I was working for the American Indian Movement. This was just one of the hazards of trying to function as a mediator. He began questioning me extensively. I asked him to check me out; I knew the Indians had their own ways of verifying information. Finally, I said, "Dennis, I have heard you say that you were willing to die here in Wounded Knee for what you believe. You've got to know that I'm willing to die for what I believe." After a few more questions, he took me across the road to security headquarters. On the way, I remembered the letter to the leaders of the American Indian Movement signed by the parents of the young people who had been killed at Kent State. The families had collected fifty-five dollars among themselves which they asked me to take to Wounded Knee in order to pay for some human need. I handed Dennis the money and the letter which began, "We the victims and the parents of the victims of the Kent State University shooting on May 4, 1970, pass on this token amount to help in some small way."

The large room in security headquarters was filled with more than a hundred young men, sitting crosslegged on the floor, all armed and listening to a security briefing. Mr. Banks asked me to stand on a tabletop, pointed up to me, and said to the group, "This man represents the National Council of Churches. I don't want you to shoot at him or other identifiable NCC representatives. They are neutral, and they are here to help establish negotiations and prevent bloodshed. Let them pass freely through the roadblocks and don't hassle them." The next day, I saw a sign in the community building which said, "Don't shoot at NCC observers. They are neutral."

I received a telephone call telling me that the chief negotiator for the government was being replaced. The new one was to be Assistant Attorney General Harlington Wood, now a federal judge in the Southern District of Illinois. Wood wanted me to work closely with him, I was told. He would call me when he arrived.

The next morning, March 13, he sent word that he wanted to see me. His first comment was, "I want to talk to them as soon as possible." I left immediately for Wounded Knee to see if there was any chance of setting up negotiations again. Within minutes of arriving in the occupied village, I was in discussion with Dennis Banks, Russell Means, Clyde Bellecourt, Carter Camp, Pedro Bissonette, Vernon Long, and several other local Wounded Knee residents.

I told them that Wood had brought a new proposal and that he wanted to talk with them as soon as possible. They agreed to talk with him on one condition. He was to come into Wounded Knee. The discussion would have to be in the small house in which we were then sitting. It was a sizeable challenge—Wood was to come down inside their territory and be in their custody during the talks.

It was 10:30 A.M. They proposed that he come for the discussion at 1:00 P.M. That didn't give much time for consideration. I drove the eighteen miles back to Pine Ridge, believing that such a counterproposal would be rejected. Until that time, negotiating sessions had been held in a tepee or in a bus in the demilitarized zone. I didn't believe that an assistant attorney general would actually go inside where he could possibly be taken hostage.

Arriving at Wood's office in the BIA building in Pine Ridge, I hesitated to make the offer. However, after I explained the proposed arrangement, he leaned back in his chair for only a moment before replying, "I presume that you will drive me out. You can pick me up at 12:30 P.M."

I dashed over to the rectory for a bowl of soup and telephoned Wounded Knee to let them know we were coming. When I returned to the BIA at 12:25 P.M., the chief of the United States marshals, Wayne Colburn, and the special agent in charge, Joseph Trimbach, were waiting for me in Wood's office. They asked pointedly, "Can you guarantee the life of this man?" referring to the assistant attorney general. I had to reply that I could not guarantee his life—or my own—but I said that the leadership in Wounded Knee had assured safe conduct for Wood and that I trusted their word. The federal officials were very uneasy. "We advise you not to go," they said to Mr. Wood. His reply made it clear that he was determined to get negotiations started again and that going into Wounded Knee seemed to be the only way. Colburn and Trimbach turned back to me, "You realize that if Mr. Wood is injured in any way, or held as a captive, there would be international as well as national repercussions?" The question needed no answer. With those words, Mr. Wood and I left.

As we drove out Highway 18, turned left on Big Foot Trail, and proceeded toward the federal roadblock, I noticed across the seat that the assistant attorney general intermittently clasped and opened his hands. He was nervous. So was I, and I began to wonder whether the plan would work. At the federal roadblock (RB-1), an extraordinary number of agents and marshals were on duty. When we stopped momentarily, several of them reached through the open car window to grip Mr. Wood's hand. They acted as if they were saying good-by.

When we reached the Indian roadblock, four young men stepped from behind the burned-out vehicles, leveled their rifles at us, and signaled us to stop. We were twenty-five yards from the checkpoint. One of them walked toward our car and told us to get out. I had expected to drive on through the roadblock and go immediately to the house where the meeting was to take place. We were more than a quarter-mile away. What had gone wrong? Had I made a mistake?

We got out of the car. The other Indians advanced, then stepped to either side of us, and led us behind the barricade. Stepping around the hulks of demolished trucks, we noticed that all of the top leadership was there—waiting. They extended their hands and gave warm words of welcome. A security force surrounded us to protect Wood, and they escorted us on foot to the house. Two young men on horses led the procession, and guards at the sides of the road saluted us. The leadership had pulled out every bit of protocol they could.

As we walked the distance to the meeting place, there was a continuous flow of banter from the Indians—beautifully appropriate humorous comments. The procession seemed designed to relieve tension and allow everyone to get acquainted. By the time we arrived at our meeting place, there was an easy stream of conversation. The discussion began without any hesitation and continued for nearly two and one-half hours. Wood listened attentively, answered questions directly, and suggested that he believed there were many negotiable points. He would make further contact after he checked with Washington.

Wood's going into Wounded Knee was a turning point. It sealed the government's commitment to a negotiated settlement. Wood's warmth and the Indians' openness illustrated that an agreement was possible.

Driving out of Wounded Knee late that afternoon, we realized that we had stayed much longer than expected. When we reached the federal roadblock, there were obvious expressions of relief from the officials. The special agent in charge for the FBI asked Wood, "How did you get along? Were you all right?"

Wood answered with a smile, "They guarded me better than you do."

Some were disappointed to learn that negotiations might possibly succeed. Those who had opposed any kind of settlement were visibly upset. Since the National Council of Churches had arranged the negotiating session, Mr. Wilson made the NCC the target of his displeasure. At his direction on March 16 the tribal court of the Pine Ridge Reservation "ordered, adjudged, and decreed that all members of the National Council of Churches and all non-members of the Oglala Sioux Tribe who are not residents of the Pine Ridge Reservation are hereby ordered to leave the Pine Ridge Reservation immediately. If they fail to leave, the Tribal Police are ordered to escort them to the nearest reservation line and they are further ordered not to return unless authorization is given by the Tribal Government."

The order was signed by the superintendent of the Bureau of Indian Affairs, a division of the Department of Interior. However, Assistant Attorney General Wood asked me only to reduce the number of persons working under NCC supervision. Immediately nearly twenty-five persons who had been transporting food, medicine, and sanitation supplies, providing for the rotation of volunteer doctors and nurses, and acting as observers for the NCC left the reservation. Only a few of us remained, but we continued working nearly around-the-clock to carry out assignments which had been agreed to by the government and by the Indians inside Wounded Knee.

Finally, in what appeared to be an effort to deal with the tribal chairman and appease him, Mr. Wood asked all persons working with the National Council of Churches—except myself—to leave the reservation. "I want you to stay," he said, "and I'm going to keep you here if I have to have you sworn in as a United States marshal and then assign you as a chaplain." I don't think that he had consulted the marshals before he made that statement. Anyway, I was clearly aware that the only appropriate role for me was as a minister of the church—with the support of the United Methodist bishop and the National Council of Churches. I could not function as an official of the United States government; neither could I work as a representative of the American Indian Movement.

Whenever I drove beyond the federal roadblock, I tied a white handkerchief to the radio antenna, just as Mr. Terronez had done on the first night. After a while the Indians tied a red cloth to my antenna so that as I drove back and forth between the lines both white and red improvised pennants fluttered from the car—symbols of the mediating role we were endeavoring to perform.

Late one night while driving up Big Foot Trail between the two roadblocks, I badly needed my handkerchief. I had a heavy cold and a deep cough, picked up in the bitter weather. I stopped the car, climbed out, and untied the handkerchief—no longer white, just tattered and gray. I needed to use it nevertheless. I drove on toward the federal roadblock and was stopped. An agent shone a flashlight on my face and then onto the car's radio aerial. Observing that only the red cloth remained, he commented as he waved me through, "Well, reverend, it looks like you've gone all the way over."

It must have seemed that way in spite of efforts to maintain a neutral stance. A memorandum to Harlington Wood from the Department of the Army, Headquarters 82nd Airborne Division at Fort Bragg, North Carolina, later introduced in court, began, "Your [Wood's] first order of business was to negotiate law enforcement aspects of the problem while that of the Indians was to air grievances against Tribal Chief Wilson and local BIA officials. Reverend Adams set it up that way since you [Wood] indicated a possible early return to Washington and Adams is sympathetic to AIM's point of view that the Oglala Sioux have been unduly abused at Pine Ridge. In short, the Indians were performing for the wrong audience. DOI [Department of Interior] should have been present."

Of course, we tried to have DOI officials present at the negotiating sessions, but it seemed to me that they were not always present because of pressures from the Bureau of Indian Affairs and the tribal chairman. The memo clarifies the dilemma in which we found ourselves and the confusion in which we worked. Every step was visible, very visible, but could be easily misinterpreted.

Sometimes it was not only a political loyalty that was being tested but an interpretation of the ministry. At a delicate point in the negotiations, the tribal council chairman told newsmen, "The Reverend John Adams is the most arrogant son of a bitch I ever met." The next morning at a press conference, a reporter repeated Wilson's description of me and asked, "What do you have to say to that?"

The only reply I could think of was, "I am an ordained son of a bitch." This may have sounded even more arrogant, but actually I was trying to explain that there was a necessary ministry to be performed in the face of violence. When human beings are determined to kill other human beings in order to solve social problems, there must be an insistence upon exploring every peaceful possibility. One has to fight for nonviolence.

During the next week I was followed and watched rather closely, but no step was taken to evict me from the reservation. In fact, with some off-reservation assistance, we were able to maintain a flow of supplies, as approved by the government, and initiate two more negotiating sessions held within the Wounded Knee village.

Wood returned to Washington for three days to discuss the situation with top officials from the Departments of Justice and Interior. While he was away, his staff assistants took a harder line. Again we heard, "Starve them out, freeze them out—or shoot them up." We kept working between the lines, but the whole situation was tightening.

When Wood returned, he had a specific proposal to present to those occupying Wounded Knee. He asked me to have the leaders meet him at the Indian roadblock so that he could present the best possible compromise that he had been able to arrange in Washington. The proposal was received, read, and rejected by the Indians. Nevertheless, we were able to set up another negotiating session—this one in the Tipi Chapel of the Church of God, a comparatively new building shaped like a huge tepee, located in Wounded Knee. The Home Missions office of the national headquarters of the Church of God in Anderson, Indiana, gave permission to use the chapel.

The sequence of events following Mr. Wood's return were reported in the *Christian Science Monitor*, March 21, 1973:

> . . . the Reverend John Adams looks slightly harried from his long hours of trying to avoid a repeat of the Wounded Knee massacre of 1890 that left several hundred Indians slain by federal troops.
>
> He is one of several key figures in the tense drama unfolding here. Mr. Adams representing the National Council of Churches (NCC) is a negotiator between the Indians and the federal forces surrounding Wounded Knee . . . He has played an important role in keeping talks going, no matter how tenuous or sporadic at times.
>
> Also helping shape events here is chief federal negotiator Harlington Wood, an assistant attorney general recently returned to Wounded Knee after consulting in Washington with high officials from the Departments of Justice and Interior. AIM leaders refused the government's settlement proposal. But a negotiating session was arranged the same day by the Reverend Mr. Adams, who drove Mr. Wood to Wounded Knee for the talks.

I had urged that negotiations be held immediately after the rejection of the proposal. The *Christian Science Monitor* reported the insistence:

> "Meaningful negotiation can not be delayed for whatever reason," said Mr. Adams, standing in the occupied grocery store at Wounded

Knee and surrounded by armed Indians. "It is frequently recited in this country that revolution cannot come at the end of a gun," he told Indians and newsmen. "But neither, really, does law and order, justice and stability, come at the end of a gun."

The negotiations got back on the track, but my involvement became even more controversial. The NCC was openly criticized by some government representatives. As I passed through the lobby of the BIA building one morning on my way to see Mr. Wood, one agent commented to another, loud enough for me to hear, "We could use our armored personnel carriers, but the National Council of Churches won't let us." The words were hostile, to say the least. I kept walking.

I realized that it was becoming more and more difficult for Mr. Wood to function. Not only the tribal chairman and the white ranchers in the area opposed negotiations, but there was increasing resistance from government personnel in Pine Ridge. Mr. Wood told me one morning that he was not sure how long either one of us might be able to stay. The next day, I was ejected from the reservation.

The confrontation came at the federal roadblock on Big Foot Trail. I was going in to make final arrangements for a safe conduct egress by representatives of the Six Nation Confederation (Iroquois, Mohawk, Seneca, and so on) who had been permitted to enter Wounded Knee and were ready to leave. I was stopped at the roadblock, but the federal agents stepped back and allowed the BIA police to take charge. "You have one hour to leave the reservation," one of them said. "We will take you back to the church, and we will wait while you pack. Then we will escort you to the reservation line."

The Bureau of Indian Affairs police had been following me for more than three days. The development was not unexpected. I threw all our equipment into the back of the station wagon and headed for Nebraska—one mile south. The BIA police car followed until I reached the state line. As I turned to wave them off, I noticed a large sign which read retroactively, "Welcome to South Dakota."

I drove to a trailer park in Rushville, Nebraska, where a group of five United Methodist ministers had a motor home on loan from Winnebago. After unpacking at this fall-back base for the NCC, I went to a restaurant in the small town where top government officials often ate their evening meal. I sat at a table and waited. I was watched closely from every table and booth by men in camouflaged fatigues and blue jump suits. I got up to use the coin telephone located in a hallway adjacent to the dining room. When I came out of the booth, two large men with cowboy hats and boots blocked the doorway leading to the dining area. The largest held his arm across the doorway at chest height, saying in low, slow words, "H-e-l-lo, AIM!" I waited, watching their faces and expecting them to take me out the side door, a few steps behind me. Gradually they grudgingly pulled aside and let me pass.

Wood arrived shortly, and we discussed the day's events. He was being sent back to Washington the next day but said it would be important for me to stay in the vicinity and work from the off-reservation base. "Try to be careful," he added.

Putting NCC off the Pine Ridge Reservation was only the beginning of a full-scale attack on the strategy of negotiations. The vigilante force, next focused on the Community Relations Service of the Department of Justice, for CRS, a federal conciliation service used in social conflicts, also had actively set up negotiation sessions. After NCC personnel left, CRS representatives were the only ones still passing between the lines. There were elements that clearly wanted them out. A new set of roadblocks, situated outside the federal roadblocks, suddenly appeared. Armed men, both white and Indian, refused to let CRS personnel through. This lasted about two days. Then Wayne Colburn sent a car with four marshals, armed with machine guns, with CRS personnel seated between them, to the roadblocks. As they drove up to the men, they opened the four doors, leveled their guns, and informed the vigilante force that CRS personnel were going into Wounded Knee and that they would continue going into the occupied village. That's what it took to keep negotiations moving.

In Rushville, the owner of the trailer park, an electrical contractor, was initially friendly and helpful. He let me use the telephone in his work shed throughout the first night. The next morning, however, he apologetically asked me to move the motor home out of his trailer park. He had received calls from other businessmen and the chief of police. "I'm sorry," he said, "but I have to live and work here."

We moved the motor home several miles to Chadron, Nebraska, a larger if not much friendlier community. Town talk revealed that the volunteer fire company had been in training to repel an Indian attack. At a given signal, men with rifles were to move to the tops of designated buildings.

As I got a haircut in a small shop in the center of town, the barber lectured me on the difference between "good Indians" and "bad Indians." "We never have had any trouble with *our* Indians," he said. The possessive pronoun revealed more than he knew.

During the next three nights, I heard someone moving around outside my motor home, parked at the Pony Trailer Court. The copper waterline, leading from the motor home to the trailer court's water system, was snapped. The next night a rock was thrown through a front window. No one actually suggested that I leave town, however.

I did not go into Wounded Knee again, but through couriers and by telephone I was able to stay in direct contact with both the Indian leaders in the occupied village and friendly government personnel in Pine Ridge. Sometimes Indians from Wounded Knee would come to the motor home to give reports. Occasionally, I would travel ninety miles to the Rosebud Sioux reservation for meetings. We opened a second NCC base in Rapid City, South Dakota, in a small house trailer, parked in the backyard of the United Methodist district superintendent, Preston Brown. I traveled between Chadron and Rapid City, working with ministers and priests in both cities and asked intermedaries to continue working on the problems which emerged day by day in Wounded Knee.

In early April I spent five days back in Washington, D.C. An April 5 agreement signed by government representatives and leaders from the Wounded Knee village provided for a meeting between White House officials and a small group of Indians from Wounded Knee. We traveled quickly to Washington to arrange for hotel rooms and meals, the cost of which was paid by church contributions.

The meeting with White House officials on April 8 never took place. That phase of negotiations collapsed as soon as it reached Washington. While the Indians waited—and waited—in their rooms in the Statler Hilton Hotel, they decided that the proposed talks were designed more as a mechanism to disarm the people in Wounded Knee than as a forum to deal with substantive issues and real grievances. The scene shifted back to Pine Ridge, and the negotiations had to be started all over. I went back to Rapid City.

Within the next month government forces and Indian occupants of Wounded Knee alternated between firefights and discussions. On April 17 an Indian, Frank Clearwater, received a serious head wound from federal gunfire. He lingered in a Rapid City hospital for more than a week before he died on April 25. Two days later an Oglala Sioux veteran of Vietnam, Buddy Lamont, was killed as he manned an Indian bunker. Rapid City pastors and I met with the families. NCC funds were used for the funeral expenses of both men.

On May 5 a final agreement was signed nearly two months after the NCC sponsored agreement had been accepted on March 8. In the interim an additional fifty thousand rounds of ammunition had been fired, a United States marshal was paralyzed from the waist down, two Indians were killed, eleven other persons were wounded, and several buildings were destroyed. Yet negotiations *did* continue, and ultimately a meeting was scheduled for May 17–18 between White House aides and the traditional chiefs.

When the tired, frustrated Indians were bused out of Wounded Knee to Rapid City, the western South Dakota town reacted with considerable concern. The National Council of Churches had another task to perform in order to relieve the anxiety of citizens and officials who wanted the Indians to move out of town quickly. That was exactly what the Indians wanted to do, but they needed bus fares, automobile repairs, and gasoline money. We arranged for the purchase of auto parts, chartered buses for larger groups going to Oklahoma and the state of Washington, and ran a traveler's aid for individuals. Within days all but a few of the Indians who had been involved in Wounded Knee and who had been released on bail or on their own recognizance had left Rapid City.

The National Council of Churches, through several persons representing it, performed a variety of roles throughout the Wounded Knee confrontation. Only a few have been described in the preceding pages. Looking back, I am convinced that one of the most important roles was being the target of those opposed to a negotiated solution. I mentioned that evaluation to an Associated Press reporter who interviewed me after the final agreement was signed. The next day, May 11, 1973, the front page headline of the Rapid City *Journal* declared, "Spokesman Says NCC 'Scapegoat.' "

The article continued, "The National Council of Churches (NCC) has been a kind of scapegoat for ministering to some of those involved in the seizure of Wounded Knee, S.D., says a spokesman for the organization. 'A scapegoat was needed, and that's not bad,' said Rev. John P. Adams."

Perhaps the church served a real purpose in strongly advocating a negotiated settlement at the outset and then being offered as a sacrifice to those who demanded a more forceful solution. The NCC left, but the negotiations continued.

When Father Pierce was allowed back into Wounded Knee after the occupation ended, he found that the Messiah Mission Episcopal Church had been used for target practice by some of the Indians. The wall behind the altar was pock-marked. A two-foot brass cross had some twenty-five indentations, probably from .22 caliber fire, and three holes from larger slugs. Father Pierce wrote in a letter, "Looking at that cross I could only think that it says more than it did before. It says that when Christians take a stand they get shot at, and that's where we ought to be."

Rev. Kent Millard, Father Pierce, Sister Hawk, and others organized a Pine Ridge Church Response Fund which received contributions from churches in South Dakota, North Dakota, and throughout the United States. The funds were used to help repair and winterize homes and to replace furniture and other household goods lost in the confrontation. Eighty Mennonite Disaster Service Volunteers worked for a two-month period, assisting more than twenty-five families.

When I was on the Pine Ridge Reservation, I heard one Washington-based government official after another say, "I have learned a lot since I've come here." That learning must spread and penetrate so that a nation can be motivated to bring justice to native Americans.

In a message to Congress on July 8, 1970, President Richard Nixon said:

> The first Americans—the Indians—are the most deprived and most isolated minority group in our nation. On virtually every scale of measurement—employment, income, education, health—the condition of the Indian people ranks at the bottom.
>
> This condition is the heritage of centuries of injustice. From the time of their first contact with European settlers, the American Indians have been oppressed and brutalized, deprived of their ancestral lands and denied the opportunity to control their own destiny.

The president then itemized some of the conditions under which American Indians live:

> Unemployment rates run as high as 80% on some reservations. The average unemployment rate on reservations is 40%.
>
> 80% of reservation Indians have an income which falls below the poverty line.
>
> The average education for all Indians under federal supervision is six school years.
>
> Drop out rates for Indians are twice the national average.
>
> The health of Indian people lags 20 to 25 years behind that of the general population.
>
> The average age at death among Indians is 44 years, about one-third less than the national average.

Infant mortality is nearly 50% higher than the national average.

The tuberculosis rate is eight times as high.

The suicide rate is twice that of the general population.

The facts and figures indicate some of the daily violences under which American Indians live. Other statistics are constantly revealed by federal agencies.

In 1973, the Federal Trade Commission reported widespread trade and credit abuses at reservation trading posts licensed by the Bureau of Indian Affairs. On reservations surveyed in three states, the trading posts maintained prices 27 percent over the national average. There are additional costs for cashing checks and obtaining credit. A comprehensive survey by the United States Census Bureau indicated almost simultaneously that "the income of Indian families falls below that of other minority groups and far below that of the nation as a whole."[1]

The occurrence of a Wounded Knee, 1973, should not have been surprising. Vine Deloria, Jr., explained that present federal laws virtually compel Indians to provoke incidents which require the United States to respond politically.[2] At this time such activism is mainly instigated by younger Indians who are battling against the despair which permeates their communities. They are turning away from resignation and hopelessness and are engaging in political actions which soon will have to be considered soberly by the government of the United States.

Indians constitute less than .5 percent of the total population of the United States, but, according to the Bureau of Census survey, Indians are younger than the population as a whole. The median age of Indians in 1970 was twenty years, eight years younger than the national median. At the same time that the national growth was 13 percent the Indian population grew 51 percent.[3]

The significance of these statistics should not be lost. Younger

1. Washington *Post*, August, 27, 1973.

2. Vine Deloria, Jr., *Behind the Trail of Broken Treaties* (New York: Dell Publishing Company), p. 145.

3. Washington *Post*, August 27, 1973.

Indians, among whom the commitment for social justice is discernibly deep, are increasing in number while their impatience is also growing. In many instances they have been joined by the elderly traditional members of the tribes who live in isolated areas of the reservations, away from the BIA compounds, and whose views are rarely recognized by the government.

The Wounded Knee occupation of 1973 was a smoke signal which should have sent a clear message to white Americans: There are desperate needs among Native Americans, and desperate steps will be taken to make those needs known and to demand help in meeting them. The federal government's own statistics confirm the human need, but a rising generation of Indians has begun to dramatize what the statistics have only vaguely revealed.

For more than two years the federal government prosecuted the nearly one hundred fifty persons who were charged with crimes related to the confrontation at Wounded Knee in 1973. Trials were held in Sioux Falls, Rapid City, Omaha, Council Bluffs, St. Paul, Cedar Rapids, and Denver.

In the Omaha trial, United States district judge Warren K. Urbom issued a memorandum and order which denied an Indian motion to dismiss charges on the grounds that their treaty rights were violated. However, in his memorandum he clarified the dilemma which Indians now confront and the challenge which White Americans now face.

Judge Urbom wrote: "It cannot be denied that official policy of the United States until at least the late 19th Century was impelled by a resolute will to control substantial territory for its westward-moving people. Whatever obstructed the movement, including the Indians was to be—and was—shoved aside, dominated, or destroyed. Wars, disease, treaties pocked by duplicity, and decimation of the buffalo by whites drove the Sioux to reservations, shriveled their population and disemboweled their corporate body. They were left a people unwillingly dependent in fact upon the United States.

"It is an ugly history. White Americans may retch at the recollection of it.

"Feeling what *was* wrong does not describe what *is* right. Anguish about yesterday does not alone make wise answers for tomorrow. Somehow, all the achings of the soul must coalesce and with the wisdom of the mind develop a single national policy for governmental action."

The judge advised the Indians that the court was the wrong forum in which to gain relief for their sovereignty grievances. He suggested the legislature, for it is "more likely to reflect the conscience and wisdom of the people."

However, if the conscience of the people is to be reflected in the voting of their legislative representatives, then that conscience must be aroused. The conscience of white America—churchgoing white America—will be the deciding factor in determining the response which the nation makes to the one-half of one percent of the population which is Indian, which has suffered historic injustice and now cries for help and appeals for hope.

Fortunately there are Indians who, by making real personal sacrifices, will not let our consciences rest. They keep calling to us to awaken and answer their cries for help. When we respond to their needs and become attentive to our national responsibility, we can begin to develop the kind of wisdom needed both to influence the legislatures and to effect a new national policy.

13

"Thou Shalt Listen"

Further accounts could be written including the response made to the textbook controversy in Kanahwa County, West Virginia or to the hospital workers strike in Pikeville, Kentucky. One could describe the help given in peacefully ending the occupation of the Alexian Brothers Novitiate by the Menominee Warrior Society in Gresham, Wisconsin.

However, it is time to stop and reflect. This is important particularly because of the prevalent weariness with protest. As one man said it, "I'm tired of their demonstrations and demands!"

It is true that after several years of movements and marches, demonstrations and confrontations, the white American public seems to be immunized to protests. Actually, the reluctance was there at the beginning. A majority were tired of the protests almost before they had begun. A considerable number however, were open to hearing the grievances clearly in order to do something about them. Now many of these people have become tired as well.

The fatigue has not always come from the heavy investment of resources or depletion of energy expended in the pursuit of justice. As the little sign which former Attorney General Ramsey Clark had on his desk said: "It is easy to do nothing and then take a rest." We gave a little and became very tired.

Weariness set in as our consciousness was expanded and as our consciences were aroused. We learned more about discrimination and deprivation than we were prepared to accept or upon which we thought we were able to act. We did not realize how much we had depended upon the quiet apathy and submission of the silent sufferers in our society. Protesters, armed with facts and figures, often from the government itself, graphically portrayed what the larger society had so conveniently and comfortably disregarded. The suffering became real—the statistics began to bleed—the facts began to stack all around us. The awakening was rude. As one person put it, "I'm more aware than I can bear." The challenges were too many and too great. We could not tolerate the pain of knowing about the suffering which others could no longer endure. We tried to go back to sleep. We tried to blink at our awareness and desensitize our consciences.

The process reminds us of the New York executive who quit his job, taking his family by Yugoslav freighter to the Canary Islands to live. He commented in a newspaper article: "I'm tired. I'm tired of my job. All I want to do is lie around and eat bananas." The wife explained: "It will be pleasant to bury my head in the sand for a while. In Manhattan I saw too many things I'd rather not see, like poverty, prejudice, and human beings being mean to each other. It's too realistic. Too hard to take." So the man and his wife and their two small sons sailed to the Canary Islands. "Frankly, it sounded like the last place in the world," the former business executive said.

A hard reality has been forced upon us and, no doubt, one of the real temptations is to try to get away from it all.

Within the church some have wanted to use the gospel of Jesus Christ as a means of escaping a world in which the wrongs were too real and the suffering too near. So the gospel has been miniaturized, privatized, and individualized to the point that it could serve as an escape hatch. The words of Jesus, "I am the way," were altered to read, "I am the way out." "Jesus Christ is the same yesterday, today, and tomorrow" were words that were interpreted as, "Jesus Christ wants everything today the way it was yesterday without allowing for any changes for tomorrow." Thus, the church has frequently found itself reverently blessing the status quo, with its injustices and its structured violence. In many instances the church has become more of a comfort station than a powerhouse.

But the Lord calls us to a greater discipleship than compliance with the oppression and exploitation of the world. He calls us to take risks and to make sacrifices which would permit us to be channels of God's intention right here on this earth. It's a serious call.

A few years ago Britain's foremost Shakespearean actor, Sir Laurence Olivier, in an interview conducted by Kenneth Harris of the *London Observer*, was asked about the satisfactions he derived from acting. Sir Lawrence replied: "The great parts—you've no idea how they devour you. You're playing Othello, God! You give it all you've got. The author says to you: You've given it all you've got? Good. Now, more, good! You've done that? Now more! More . . . more! more! MORE! M-O-R-E! and your heart and your guts and your brain are pulp, and their part feeds on them. Acting great parts devours you. Great parts are cannibals. It is a dangerous game."

The gospel of Jesus Christ is not something to take lightly. It makes demands. The Lord has requirements for discipleship. We give a little and the Lord asks for more—then more—and more! Our mind and our heart and our spirit want to be freed. Our following him is more dangerous than we expected. It is a part that feeds on us. Yet—and the learning of it seems to come only when we are reduced to the point of near fatal fatigue and desperate disillusionment—WE ARE FED. The words: "My strength is sufficient for you" begin reflecting a reality. Jesus Christ asks everything that we have, so it is said, but he gives us back everything, so we learn.

We may become tired but there's one thing we can always assume. God is present where there is human need, and the spirit of God is especially active where the issues of justice and freedom are at stake. This little credo, so simple on the surface, has a profound dimension to it. It means that God enters the unlikely places, calls improbable persons, assembles unpromising resources, and then works the will of His spirit. This is not a new message, of course. The Bible is filled with examples in which God has acted in precisely this way among the Hebrew people and within the community of early Christians. Perhaps we should reconsider the role played in our society by those we call radical and militant, agitators and troublemakers.

In the letter to the Hebrews (13:2 KJV) it is written: "Let brotherly love continue. Be not forgetful to entertain strangers for thereby some have entertained angels unawares." As we've been forced to attend the so-called militant protester, we may have heard the voice of a prophet without knowing it.

In early 1976, a group of lay persons, pastors and theologians, convened by the Boston Industrial Mission, issued the Boston Affirmations including this statement of faith: "God chooses strangers, servants and outcasts to be witnesses and to become a community of righteousness and mercy. Beyond domination and conflict, God hears the cry from the oppressed and works vindication for all. God forms 'nobodies' into 'somebodies' and makes known the law of life."

How amazing it is that God takes whatever fragments of commitment and cooperation any of us give and then expands and shapes them until they reflect a loving will. I must confess there was a time when I believed that this phenomenon was confined to the community of faith, that the activity of God's spirit was channeled exclusively through the church. Until I was thrown into the movements for human justice during the past several years, I did not know how mistaken I was. At first I could not admit it for I was so much a part of the church. I began to realize that what we had been talking about in the church was being acted out sacrificially within movements often emphatically secular.

I was struck with the truth that, "God works where He wills." God does not wait on the church, but uses optional channels to raise the issues boldly when the church speaks timidly and acts hesitantly. This is part of the Good News. God moves in his own way in our day.

Such witnessing can be threatening. The threat is understandable if the account of Jesus' appearance in his hometown synagogue is read in the Gospel according to Luke (Luke 14:14–30 NEB). Jesus, "armed with the power of the Spirit," went to Nazareth and on the Sabbath day stood up and read from the Prophet Isaiah:

> The Spirit of the Lord is upon me
> because He has anointed me;
> He has sent me to announce good
>   news to the poor,
> to proclaim release for prisoners
>   and recovering of sights of the blind;
> to let the broken victims go free,
> to proclaim the year of the Lord's favor.

Following the reading Jesus was admired by his hometown friends when he declared, "Today, in your very hearing this text has become true." The warm regard ended abruptly, however, when Jesus used two examples from history to show how God had worked his purpose from outside Israel, the community of faith. Then his former friends forced him out of the town and attempted to push him off a cliff.

It is not easy for the community of faith to be confronted with the truth by those who are not among the faithful. One of the first impulses within the church in our time was to do to the leaders of the movements what Jesus' hometown friends had tried to do to him. The church often joined with others in attempts to have leaders thrown out. We shouted, "America, love it or leave it." But they have not left and cry back at us, "America, change it or lose it." There were efforts made to discredit the movement leaders by agencies of the government and often unwittingly the church's climate sanctioned such acts.

The most severe rejection of God's new witnesses came by labeling all efforts for social change and all of the leaders working for social justice as Communistic. It was a tag thrown about so easily, it rather senselessly gave the impression that only Communists wanted justice in our society. Yet, the Spirit of the Lord which creates justice, shows mercy, and makes all things new. Jesus Christ redeems the soul of the society.

The church can derive a clue as to how God works in society through recognizing the essential message being delivered by the movements for justice. What are the grievances that are being expressed? What are the human needs which are exposed? What are the issues which are raised? What are the obstacles which are discovered? What is the power that can move them? What new opportunities are opened?

Of course, not every movement leader is divinely ordained nor is every movement directed by the Lord's Spirit. But the potential is there and God may be speaking and we should not turn away without listening. The church needs to identify with the movements for justice and human liberation, wherever possible, in order to learn what the Lord may be saying and doing.

The Central Committee of the World Council of Churches commended a statement on "Violence, Non-violence and the Struggle for Social Justice" to the member churches for study, comment, and action in 1973. It recommended to the General Secretary of the WCC that "the possibility of developing new kinds of crisis intervention ministries, in close relationship with churches in such crisis areas," be explored. It was a renewed recognition that the ministries of the church need to be attached directly and strongly to the struggles of the poor and the oppressed, particularly in the critical places and during the crucial events in which their destinies are so radically and rapidly shaped.

In crisis intervention ministries, of course, the church cannot enter now with the easy assumption that it will be the grand peacemaker or the noble reconcilor. As Dr. Jürgen Moltmann, professor of theology at Tubingen University, said to the World Student Conference at Turku, Finland, in 1968:

> Conflicting parties have become tired of abstract appeals to their conscience and weary of verbal sermons on morality. They do not expect to resolve their conflicts with the aide of a transcendental wisdom of the church.

Indeed the church is often seen as one of the forces of resistance which must be overcome if social change is to take place and social justice achieved.

When the American Indian Movement ended its 1975 annual convention, held on a mesa six miles southwest of Farmington, New Mexico, it issued a report naming the three major enemies of the Indian people. They were: (1) the institution of the Christian church; (2) anti-Indian education; and (3) the United States government—its agents, the Department of Interior, and the Bureau of Indian Affairs. The Church was not just listed as *an* enemy but as the number one enemy.

As the World Council of Churches statement on "Violence, Non-violence and the Struggle for Social Justice" appropriately declared:

> Churches and Christians are realizing that they have too seldom been on the side of the poor and the oppressed. They have too often supported the powers of an unjust social order. They often have profited from the poverty of others. They have in the past used force when they were in power against those who differed from them in belief or ideology. Their first word to this problem must be one of repentance.

Repentance is not easy. It is not easy for an individual and it is no easier for the church. There are all kinds of evasive tactics which the human spirit will take to avoid repentance, and the church can use these as well as any person. Yet there are times when church has made its confession.

In the early 1950s, the Council of the Protestant Church in Germany, stating its desire to share in the responsibility of the German nation during World War II, declared to visiting representatives of the World Council of Churches:

> Through us has endless suffering been brought to many peoples and countries. What we have often born witness to before our congregations, that we declare in the name of the whole church. True we have struggled for many years in the name of Jesus Christ against a spirit which has found its terrible expression in the National Socialist regime of violence, but we accuse ourselves for not witnessing more courageously, for not praying more faithfully, for not believing more joyously and for not loving more ardently.

The first word was repentance.

In reference to the American Indians, the Lutheran Council in the U.S.A. spoke these words:

> We have been repeatedly reminded and confronted by the realities of the Indian fragmentation, starvation and confinement. Our declaration of "freedom for all" and "love for neighbor" have been hollow words lacking integrity of positive life actions. Voices of protest within the Indian community have been largely silenced by inattention or organizational hangups, and tactics which promise action later on. . . . We are less human, our nation is poor; the family of God in Jesus Christ is hurting because of the continuing anguish which is carried by Indian people.

Without such repentance there is no sense of the collective responsibility which we have for the social sins of the past and for the social injustices of the present. Yet through repentance there flows the power of forgiveness; it is this reality which enables us to work again for God's justice among human beings. Perhaps our tiring of protest was not just a matter of vastly expanded consciousness or an overly aroused conscience after all. We may have been burdened with the sense of our social sins without any freeing of our collective spirit by God's own sacrificial forgiveness.

Through the movements for social justice God may be calling us to repentance both within the church and within the nation. In 1975, the Minnesota Catholic Conference, while admitting that "missionary efforts frequently contributed to the disruption of Indian cultures by undermining the peoples' pride in self, community and heritage" also rightfully declared in a statement entitled "A New Beginning": "We look to the past in order to learn. If we remain enslaved to the past we remain guilt-ridden. Our need is to be free to act reasonably and responsibly in the present."

Through forgiveness God frees the church to use what it has learned from the past to assume responsibilities in the present. Repentance is an act of learning, forgiveness an empowering one.

Some may fear that the church, like Alice in Wonderland,

would drown in its own tears if it actively engaged in repentance for the social sins of the nation. They are so many. Yet it is precisely through the recognition of responsibility for the past that there is furnished strength to serve in the present and the possibility of being used in shaping the future. Repentance is not a delaying tactic. It is a spiritual necessity. Forgiveness follows.

When the church identifies with the movements for social justice, it cannot be with the proud confidence that it has the ready answers to the issues at stake. But rather there must be a sense of shared responsibility for the conditions which lie at the root of any crisis and with the faith that justice will prevail.

The church must identify with the struggles in practical ways. At the World Council of Churches special consultation on human rights in St. Pölten, Austria, in October 1974, it was suggested that the churches could assist in resisting oppression by "making pastoral visits to particular situations as an act of solidarity of Christians throughout the world with victims of violations and those struggling for the defence of human rights."

At the least the church must get near enough to the struggles to discover what its ministry ought to be. When the church shares the vulnerabilities of the victims of violations of human rights, it begins to find the specific steps that it can take to re-establish those rights. We can begin to discover the resources which God has placed in our hands and which can be used in healing ways. Forgiveness becomes operational.

The church cannot support persons or groups which are simply protesting against those who are protesting against injustice. As long as injustice exists in our society there will be protests. Unmet needs have to be dramatized. Unfulfilled promises should be highlighted. Suffering must be made plain and a clear light should be thrown on exploitation.

The church can not give aid and comfort to persons or groups who would muffle the cries of those in need or who would shut their eyes to the injustices of our society. When it was suggested to Jesus that he quiet his disciples, he replied, "I tell you if my Disciples keep silence, the very stones will cry out" (Luke 19:40 NEB).

The disciples could not be quieted in their praise of him. Neither can we silence those whom God would use to call us to greater faithfulness in the society in which we live. When we try to quiet them, God will use other voices. But when we listen to them, he will use us as well.